D0804009

don't take me home those people hate me

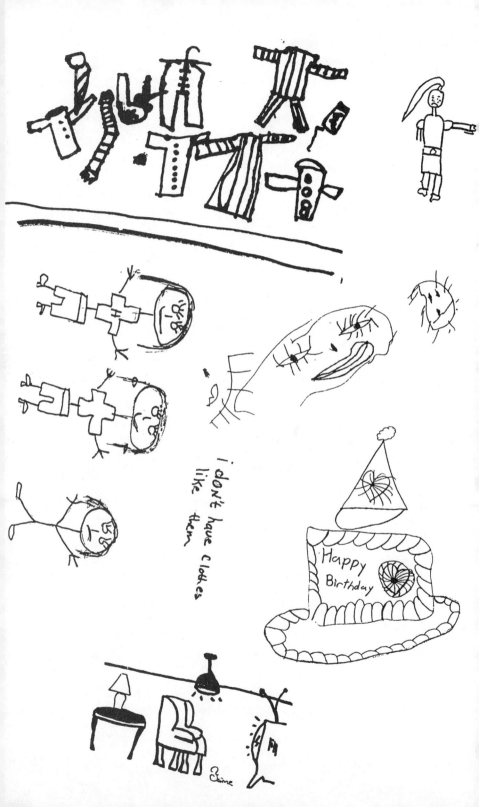

i don't have clothes like them

HOW TO SAVE THE CHILDREN

AMY HATKOFF

•

KAREN KELLY KLOPP

A FIRESIDE BOOK   PUBLISHED BY
SIMON & SCHUSTER
NEW YORK   LONDON   TORONTO
SYDNEY   TOKYO   SINGAPORE

F

FIRESIDE
Simon & Schuster Building
Rockefeller Center
1230 Avenue of the Americas
New York, New York 10020

Designed by Bonni Leon
Manufactured in the United States of America

10   9   8   7   6   5   4   3   2   1

Library of Congress Cataloging-in-Publication Data
Hatkoff, Amy.
      How to save the children / Amy Hatkoff, Karen Kelly Klopp.
         cm.
      "A Fireside book."
      Includes bibliographical references and index.
      1. Child welfare—United States—Handbooks, manual, etc.
   2. Child welfare—United States—Directories.   I. Klopp, Karen
   Kelly.   II. Title.
   HV741.H36   1992
   362.7'1'0973—dc20   92–21870
                                                           CIP

ISBN 0-671-76997-9

This book is dedicated to the beauty and spirit of children
everywhere.

It is written in awe of their ability to hold on, to persevere, and
to overcome.

It is both a plea and a testament of faith that we will not wait
a moment longer to reach out to them.

It is also written in honor of the hundreds of thousands of people
in this country who have already opened their hearts to a child in
need and in the hope that this will be done for every child.

ACKNOWLEDGMENTS

We would like to thank all the organizations and programs that appear in this book for their willingness to participate and their support of the project. Everyone we spoke with was tremendously helpful and generous with their time, information, and advice.

We would like to thank Marian Wright Edelman, founder and president of the Children's Defense Fund, for writing the foreword, thereby gracing this book with her profound vision and her powerful conviction that the well-being of every child be ensured.

We extend a special thanks to Donna Jablonski, director of publications at the Children's Defense Fund, for guiding the project along and applying an expert eye to the manuscript; to Mark Riley, director of the Child Welfare League of America's Children's Campaign, for support and encouragement from the very start of the project, and to Maura Wolf, youth service coordinator at the Points of Light Foundation, for providing terrific contacts and counsel on the manuscript.

We'd also like to thank Ann Kittlaus from The Food Research and Action Center; Janet Cox from the National Association from Partners in Education; Gail Kong and Cathyrn Berger-Kaye from StarServe, and Winifred Brown from the Mayor's Voluntary Action Center for their expertise and assistance.

We thank John Bess, Alfonso Wyatt, and Dr. Michael Carrera, whose work and dedication to children and youth in need have been sources of inspiration, motivation, and enlightenment.

We'd like to thank Nancy Love, our agent, for believing in the book from the beginning and in our ability to do it; Sheridan Hay, our editor, for her support, encouragement, and expertise as well as her commitment to the book and her belief in its possibilities; and Simon and Schuster's Fireside imprint, our publisher, for putting these words into print. A special thanks to Ricki Stern and Will

Rexer for affirming that visions and ideas can become realities and for helping to make them so. We especially thank Nancy McCullough for her talents in organizing, arranging, and editing the manuscript—and her commitment to it all. We want to thank John Klopp for his counsel, humor, and encouragement; Jake and Adam Klopp for their grown-up patience and understanding; Sandra Lewis for her intelligence and her ability to do it all with ease; Corey Oser for her wonderful spirit and unique talent in extracting information; Susan Patricof, Robyn Scholer, Deborah Kirsch, and Susan Wolf for the hours they spent listening to the manuscript and their insightful input; Craig Hatkoff for his faith, encouragement, and advice; James Patricof for expert technical advice and counsel; Mickey Ward and Kathleen Wolf for their help with the art-work; Gloria Baker and Lois Zenkel for their magic with the camera; Andrew Turetsky for always having the time to help out; Victor Capital Group for sharing resources; and Linda Gusler for her time.

We'd like to thank our mothers, Doris Hatkoff and Mildred Kelly, for cheering us on and helping to make this possible. In memory of Leon Hatkoff, Amy would like to acknowledge his ever present support. His values, sensitivity and life-long belief in the "underdog" laid the groundwork for this book. Karen would especially like to thank her late father, James B. Kelly, for his inspiration. His straightforward yet compassionate approach to life was a constant guide through this project. She would also like to thank Dick and Louise Klopp for their moral support.

And last but never least, our thanks go out to all the children we have met along the way whose cries have beckoned us and whose spirit and potential have galvanized us.

C O N T E N T S

F O R E W O R D

by Marian Wright Edelman

Every morning, as we wake up, one hundred thousand American children wake up homeless.

Every thirteen seconds, as we get out of bed, an American child is reported abused or neglected.

Every thirty-two seconds, about the time it takes us to walk to the kitchen and put on the coffee, an American baby is born into poverty.

Every fourteen minutes, while we shower and brush our teeth, a baby dies in America.

Every sixty-four seconds, while we lock our doors and head for work, a baby is born to a teenage mother.

And every thirteen hours, before we go back to sleep at night, an American preschooler is murdered.

Our children are being left behind. In economic opportunity and living standards, they are being left behind their parents' generation. In education, family support, and their ability to survive infancy, they have fallen behind children of other nations. The number of American children who are poor—13.4 million—is greater than the entire population of Illinois, Pennsylvania, or Florida. If Florida were devastated by a natural disaster that left all of its citizens poor, the nation would recognize a state of emergency and pull together to save the state.

It is time to apply that same national will and strength of values to saving our children.

what do america's children need?

To safeguard our children—and our nation's future—every one of us must act on their behalf. As this book shows, there are countless ways to take part in efforts to improve the lives of children. Regardless of our individual resources, we all can do something. Helping does not require wealth or great power. It takes caring, hard work, and persistence.

We can start in our homes and communities by being good role models and teachers and by donating what we can—in time, talent, or money—to effective child-serving programs.

But individual efforts alone cannot ensure that no child is left behind. It also requires firm public- and private-sector values and political participation by every citizen and the nation. No well-intentioned citizen acting alone can end child poverty. No unemployed father alone can revive the manufacturing industry in his Steel Belt hometown, and no low-income working mother can control the cost of her child's medical care. We must act collectively for children, in our communities, clubs, workplaces, and religious institutions, so that our good works increase with broad-based participation. And collectively we must demand that our government at every level place children first among the interests vying for priority treatment.

We must work together to build a national climate that makes it un-American for any child to suffer homelessness, hunger, abandonment, and the needs bred of poverty. We must redefine our idea of "national security" to include smart children rather than just smart bombs. We must insist that our nation invest in its future by investing in the children who will grow to lead it.

all american children need and deserve:

· **A Healthy Start**—basic health care for every child and pregnant woman.

· **A Head Start**—good preschool and child care to help them get ready for school, keep up in school, and prepare for the future.

· **A Fair Start**—jobs at wages that can support families, tax credits for families with children, and child support from absent parents.

we *can* act to leave no child behind

America *can* save its children. We know that investing early in children not only works, it also saves tax dollars. We know that early investment costs less than ignorance, illness, teen pregnancy, and welfare dependency.

We know that every $1.00 spent on childhood immunizations can save $10 in later medical costs; that every $1.00 spent for quality preschool education, such as Head Start, can save $4.75 in later special education, crime, welfare, and other costs; that $1.00 in Medicaid spent for a pregnant woman's comprehensive maternity care can save $3.38 in later health costs. And we know these investments make a huge and humane difference in the quality of children's lives.

America has always been a "can-do" nation. We can do what we put our minds and our national will to do. History will judge us on whether we apply that will as strongly to protecting the survival of our most precious and most vulnerable citizens—our children—as we have applied it to national efforts such as Desert Storm and the savings and loan bailout.

Speak out for children. Act and demand action. Register, vote, and let your vote be a proxy for those too young to cast their ballots. Stay informed about the status of children by contacting the Children's Defense Fund and other groups listed in this book. Inform others about how to meet children's needs. Write letters to the editor. Call and write your government representatives *regularly*. Encourage others you know to do so as well.

Together we can save our children. Together we *can* make sure that no child is left behind.

Marian Wright Edelman is founder and president of the Children's Defense Fund, 122 C Street, NW, Washington, DC 20001.

INTRODUCTION

This book was inspired by my experience working with the children at the Prince George Hotel in New York City. The Prince George was the largest welfare hotel in the world. At the time I was there, it housed more than two thousand children. I had seen many children in my career, but I had never seen anything like this. The children there personalized and gave life to every statistic or story I had ever heard of the plight of children in this country.

Living at the Prince George was like being in the front line of a battle and these were the children who took the full brunt of attacks. Gun shots went off rather routinely and drug-induced rages were a daily occurrence. Childhood took on a meaning totally different than anything I had ever associated it with. The things I took for granted about it seemed to be almost completely absent. Children at eight years were left to care for their younger siblings. Children sometimes lived with as many as six people in a room the size of a small hallway. These rooms did not have toys, books, or puzzles—any of the normal signs of childhood. Children often missed school because, in the chaos of their lives, school could not be kept as a priority. They often had only torn cotton t-shirts to wear in the middle of winter or the same dress or pants to wear day after day. Many of the children had scars on their arms and faces which I later learned came from cigarettes or even irons used as punishment. Yet, the children were magnificent. Beneath the torn clothing, the hungry faces, and the scars were children dying for love, attention, and support.

I became the director of the volunteer program. At one point there were more than two hundred individuals from the community, from all walks of life, who came to the hotel once or even twice a week to work one on one with the children. The relationships between the children and their "tutors" as they were called were inspired and magical. The children seemed to know automatically when someone had something to share with them. They soaked up the love and concern like sponges. They wanted so much to be normal children, to be a part of life, to follow a positive path. And they knew their tutors could share some of that with them.

Bridges were being built for these children and the traffic went two ways. Children were going out into the community—to museums, movies, restaurants, their tutors' offices—and members of the community were bringing their love and caring into the hotel. Some kind of miracle was beginning to happen on 28th Street.

The impact of this experience has never left me. It pointed out that there was so much we could do. If we could provide the children with love and constructive experiences, and the mothers with support and resources, we could increase the hope for their futures. The experience also showed me that people really wanted to help, and when asked, were only too willing to do so. It seemed that what people needed to get involved was a link, and the knowledge that their help was needed.

Eventually, almost everyone in my immediate world became involved in some way or another—my nephews, my brother-in-law, his running partner, my hair cutter, my aerobics teachers, people I'd meet on a train, in a restaurant. The desire to help was contagious and was spreading fast. Perhaps one of the most important connections I made at that time was with Karen, with whom I've launched many projects, including writing this book.

To me, the children at the Prince George Hotel were the unsung heroes of a war being waged in America. They withstood the deprivation, the violence, and the humiliation of their poverty and their circumstances, and still wanted to celebrate and be a part of life. To me, these children represented what was most noble about the human spirit, and they seared indefinitely in my mind the magnitude of the resilience of the human soul. I felt that if people could know these children the way I had come to know them, and recognize their capacity to help them, they would not think twice about reaching out.

This book was written to tell the story of these children and the millions like them living in America. It is born of the faith that their situation, both unacceptable and unimaginable, can and will be different, and of the conviction that it is within the capacity of each and every one of us to make it so. It is our hope that in reading this book you will be moved to join with others in our most important task, that of saving our children.

Amy Hatkoff
New York City
1992

When Amy and I sat down to talk, I was—I suspect—like many of our readers. I had no background in the social services but knew from observing my day-to-day routine in the city that life was deteriorating for a large segment of the population. I was anxious to do something to help but didn't know exactly how or what to do. Luckily for me, Amy did. Her belief in the resiliency of the human spirit and her commitment to the ideals of self-esteem and dignity for each and every person was what finally moved me to action. We decided to bring the support group started at the hotel by Amy and Lois Zenkel to area shelters. As a mother myself, I was aware of my all-encompassing effect on the well being of my children. When I was happy, they were happy. If I had a bad day, everyone suffered. We set up The Women's Group to provide respite, friendship, self-esteem, and a little fun to a group of women who sometimes seemed, even at a very young age, worn down by their lives.

We met once a week for three hours, and brought in speakers from the community to share their experience with our group. Some of our most popular sessions were with the instructors from Bank Street College, demonstrating parenting techniques. As the women spoke of their backgrounds, the drugs, the violence, the poverty, it became apparent that very often their own mothers had not been there for them. The nurturing and role modeling that all young parents need was not being passed from generation to generation. Yet they wanted their children's lives to be different than their own and they were willing to seek help to accomplish it. The chain had been broken and we were providing one of the links.

When everyone we came in contact with wanted to contribute something to "the group," I realized that this was not the exception. Most people were enthusiastic about getting involved when asked or shown how. Amy and I felt the frustration of knowing that the vast potential in the community was untapped and we committed ourselves to finding a large-scale way to link those in need with existing opportunities. This book is a result of that commitment.

From my background in conservation and wildlife films, I have seen firsthand the power of the media. As part of the movement that drew attention to the unconscionable slaughter of African elephants for their tusks and the deforestation of the Amazon rain forest for gold mining, I had to ask the question: "If we can mobilize people to save the planet, why not its children?" One of the wonderful, observable outcomes of this attention to the environment is that our children have become more responsible earth citizens than we are. Children today grow up recycling, conserving, and acknowledging the fragility of the planet. It will be the same with the care we take with our children and youth at risk. Given our support and attention, I believe these children *can* grow up to lead this country and its youth away from the destructive paths of violence, drugs, and disinterest to a positive and productive future.

Karen Kelly Klopp
New York City
1992

GETTING
STARTED

This book offers specific steps you can take to help counteract the impact of poverty and neglect on our nation's children. It is an invitation to get involved and a guide on how to do it. It is based on the premise that everyone has something to offer and is designed to help you discover what that is for you.

You might view the situation facing our young people as hopeless and feel as though there is nothing you can do to make a difference. Perhaps you feel intimidated by the prospect of getting involved, or find it hard to imagine what you personally could do. We hope this book can change your way of thinking. There are so many ways to help that you should be able to find something you feel comfortable doing and that you can make a part of your life.

We offer hundreds of suggestions ranging in complexity and level of commitment. Getting involved can mean saving your children's clothing and toys, driving a mother and a sick child to a health clinic, reading to a child, or making a call to Washington. What is important is that *everyone* develops an awareness of the problem and finds some way to be a part of the solution.

Even the smallest contributions can make a difference. You will read of Common Cents New York, a program started by Teddy Gross, in which community members "harvest" the pennies in their neighborhoods. In just one month, students of the Dalton Middle School in New York City collected $29,000 worth of pennies and change which they donated to programs for homeless children.

You can make a difference in the life of a child simply by sharing something you know or enjoy doing. You will learn of Jim Hubbard, a photojournalist, who taught one homeless boy how to use a camera. Today, through his organization, Shooting Back, growing numbers of photographers in Washington, DC, give their time to work with children, teaching them their skills and offering guidance and support.

These are just a couple of examples of what individuals and groups across the country are already doing to make things better for children. Despite the magnitude of the problem, we as a nation can be very proud of these efforts. This book heralds these programs and presents them both as models and inspirations.

how to use this book

Each chapter offers a range of suggestions that address a particular aspect of the problems facing our children. Next to the suggestions you will find an example of a program or organization that is dealing successfully or innovatively with that particular problem. There are phone numbers to call to participate in that organization's efforts. Most of the local programs cited can be replicated in your own community. The people involved in these programs will be happy to guide you in setting up your own program.

At the back of each chapter there is a comprehensive listing of national organizations to contact for more information on a particular topic, and to find out more on what you can do to make a difference in your own community. Many of these organizations have excellent journals, manuals, and guides.

The end of the book offers a section on organizations that either have branches across the country, or have data base information on programs nationwide. These organizations can give you ideas on how to get started and link you to programs in your community.

Almost every program and organization you will read about was started because one person had an idea, a solution, or something to share. We hope that as you read, you will realize that *your* ideas can become realities and that *your* concerns—when voiced—can become vehicles for change.

guidelines for understanding and interacting with children

uplifting our awareness

The way we view our children will determine how we care for them. It is important that we begin to see children "at risk" in a new light—one of respect and admiration, one of compassion and concern. These children are struggling with obstacles that to most of us are unimaginable. When we talk about children at risk, we are referring to the millions of children in this country who lack the basic necessities required for healthy growth and development. We are talking about millions of children who struggle every day simply to survive. If not provided with intervention and safety nets, these children run high risks of grim outcomes in their lives. By reaching out to these children, we can help turn their lives around. The following are some ways to increase our awareness and to open our hearts.

"Treat the person as if they were your child."
—JOHN BESS, *founder and executive director*
The Valley Youth Program of the Cathedral of St. John the Divine
New York City

• <u>Understand the circumstances of a child's life.</u>   When you see a child or a young person, try to keep in mind what may be happening in his or her life. It is not unusual for a child of seven or eight to be responsible for the meals and safety of younger siblings. It is not unusual for a child to fear for his or her *survival* when walking to school or in the neighborhood. It is not unlikely for a child to choose or be forced by the courts to leave home because of severe neglect or abuse.

· <u>Give credit where credit is due.</u> Simply being able to survive these grim circumstances takes tremendous determination, perseverance, and will. For millions of children, growing up is a heroic act. Still to be able to reach out and want to be a part of things is commendable. These children deserve praise and recognition.

· <u>See the value and potential in each child.</u> What is possible for one child to become or achieve is possible for every child—if given support and opportunities.

working one on one

Your simply being with a child and showing an interest can have a tremendous impact. People often think they won't know how to interact with a child, that they won't know what to say or do. Your presence and concern alone can be of great benefit. Often, the child can be your best guide. The following are some insights into what your interaction can impart as well as some guidelines.

· <u>Treat a child with respect.</u> Children at risk may have no one to build them up or to reflect positive self-images. They can grow up feeling terribly worthless and unwanted. Treating a child with respect and expectation can help build badly damaged self-esteem and help a child begin to feel that he or she matters—and has value.

· <u>Help a child recognize his or her abilities.</u> Point out what the child can do. You may be the first person ever to tell a child that he or she is capable or competent.

· <u>Listen to a child.</u> Most children at risk need desperately to be heard. They need the experience of a kind and caring person listening to how they feel. Your attentiveness to a child who has so many obstacles to overcome can provide great relief and a sense of being supported. Your responsiveness can also encourage a child to express his or her needs or feelings with words rather than by acting out.

• **Use positive language.** Kind, supportive, and encouraging words can do a great deal to counteract the negativity so many children must deal with daily. "I enjoy talking to you," "You are very talented," and "You look so nice" are phrases a child cannot hear often enough.

• **Communicate your belief.** Letting the child know you have faith that he or she can achieve goals can help him or her to do just that. Your communicating positive expectations can help the child to believe in his or her abilities.

• **Be consistent.** Keeping your appointment to meet with a child is very important. Your consistency and concern can help children begin to develop trust, which is essential to forming positive relationships. The converse is also true. Your not showing up can add to the many disappointments the child may have already experienced.

HELPING

WITH THE

BASICS

"Begin with your own children. Love them. Spend time with them. Guide them and be prepared to discipline them. Spark their imaginations. As a family, with your children, reach out to other children. Make helping neighbors a way of life."

—SAM BEARD, president
The American Institute for
Public Service

"People think that unless they can devote themselves like Mother Teresa, they will not make a difference; and this is not true. One person reaching out to one person can make an incredible difference, both in the life of the one being touched, and those that he touches."

—ALFONSO WYATT, vice president
Fund for the City of New York
New York City

"All children deserve the chance to be kids, to live free of poverty, illness, and fear, to explore, learn, and play, to grow up in an atmosphere of hope, expectation, and love. As grown-ups, we've got to provide them with that chance."

—DAVID SALTZMAN, executive
director
Robin Hood Foundation
New York City

H   U   N   G   E   R

How does it feel to be hungry?

" . . . like I ain't got nobody."—Kamal, age five

" . . . like nobody is taking care of me."—Harry, age seven

" . . . like I shouldn't exist."—Wilfred, age fourteen

—participants, Hunger Action Coalition

Detroit, Michigan

It is hard to imagine that in this country, so rich in resources, millions of children go hungry every day. Yet five and a half million children, or one out of every eight American children under twelve years old, is hungry. Millions more children stand to meet this fate if this problem goes unaddressed. Hunger robs children of the tools they need to develop their bodies, minds, and spirits. Impoverished beginnings will impact a child for a lifetime. A hungry child runs a high risk of illness and a poor chance of healthy growth and development. A child who is hungry cannot concentrate or do well in school. A child whose basic needs go unmet time after time is likely to give up hope. There is enough food in this country to end childhood hunger. This section offers steps we can all take to accomplish this end.

donate food from your home

Food programs across the country routinely have to turn children and families away because of shortage of supplies. If everyone simply donated cans of food from their kitchen cabinets, we could help these food programs build up their reserves and feed more children. Encourage your friends, coworkers, or classmates to join you in donating goods on a regular basis. To find a food program in your area, contact a church or synagogue or ask your local hunger program.

"Hunger is something that we always think of in terms of another country. We don't understand how terrible hunger is in this country for children. There is enough food wasted in this country to feed every child. Getting that food to those children is within each of our capacity."

—BRET SUVAL, *executive director*
City Harvest
New York City

The Campaign to End Childhood Hunger provides information and advocacy tools to hunger groups across the country. For advice or to find a program in your area, call 202-986-2200.

The Chicago Bulls ask fans to bring canned goods to one game every December to be donated to the Anti-Hunger Federation. In 1991 more than three tons of food were donated.

---

organize a food drive

Large quantities of food can be gathered through organizing a food drive. Select a program to benefit, and publicize the date and place for donations. A radio station may give you free publicity. Make your food drive a regular project. While the need is there all year round, it is especially important during the winter months, when families can be forced to choose between heating their homes or feeding their children. Ask your local food program for advice on running an innovative and effective drive.

"Congress must lead the charge to protect the most vulnerable of American citizens, our children. But this does not absolve the American people of all responsibility. Every citizen must do what he or she can. Every gesture, no matter how small, makes a difference, for only a nationwide commitment to our underprivileged children can restore their health and promise for the future."

> —*Representative* TONY P. HALL, *chairman, U.S. House of Representatives Select Committee on Hunger*

For a free pamphlet on how you can help the homeless and hungry in your neighborhood, call the Citizens Committee for New York City at 212-684-6767.

Demian, age twelve

help out in a soup kitchen

For many children, soup kitchen meals are their only source of clean and nutritious food. Help prepare and serve meals. Your kind smile can go a long way to boost a child's spirits. Contact your local church or synagogue to find a kitchen.

"Very often a child in our program will ask for food to feed their entire family. They hide food in clothing or furniture or behind a bookcase so they can retrieve it later and have enough to feed their families."
—PAM SELDEN, director
Children's-Teen Programs
Martha's Table
Washington, DC

Food & Hunger Hotline can help you start a soup kitchen or a food pantry. For more information, call 212-366-5400.

---

ask your supermarket to set up a donation bin

This is a good way to remind people about the need to help and to make it easy to do so. Help your supermarket by selecting a food program and arranging for the pickup. Many supermarkets will match customers' donations.

"There is a look of desperation that comes over the face of a child when he is hungry, cold, forgotten, or lonely . . . it is the look of fear. As caring human beings, we have an obligation to help the children. The power to make a difference in their world is at our fingertips. We only need to reach out and help."
—RICHARD F. SCHUBURT, president
and CEO
Points of Light Foundation

Through the Food Industry Crusade Against Hunger's Consumer Sharing Program, customers in almost five thousand supermarkets nationwide are invited to contribute their change to support local and global hunger programs. Encourage your store manager to participate by calling 202-429-4555.

support the efforts of a food bank

Every year, billions of dollars' worth of perfectly edible food ends up as landfill. These items have either been overproduced, or may have slight imperfections and cannot be sold. Throughout the country, a network of food banks is working with the food industry to ensure that these surplus items are channeled to hungry children and families. Find out how you can help your local food bank.

A&P Food Stores directs $10 million worth of unsalable food each year to food banks throughout the country.

Second Harvest, a national network, channels over five hundred million pounds of food and grocery products worth over $1 billion annually from the food industry to those in need. To find a food bank in your area, call 312-263-2303.

donate leftover foods or perishables

Tons of perishable foods are directed to families each month through the network of Prepared and Perishable Food Programs. Suggest that your local restaurants, supermarkets, bakeries, greengrocers, and farmers donate to this system. Any extra food you have from a party or event can be put to good use.

"We view hunger in America as a problem that can be significantly reduced. It is our hope that by supporting the distribution of nutritious food, we are helping to provide the hungry with the strength, hope, and resolve to begin the process toward self-sufficiency."

—CLEMENT E. HANRAHAN, executive director
United Parcel Service
Foundation
Atlanta, GA

adopt a food program

If you don't have the time to help hands-on, find out about having your business or social group help finance a hunger program. Everyone can pitch in a certain amount a month to a food fund. Once your group establishes a connection to a specific program, your members are more likely to become involved on a regular basis.

Cyclists Ending Hunger, a group of citizens concerned about hunger, bike across the country to raise awareness and funds. To join their efforts or to start a bike tour in your community, call 808-396-8306.

More than $3 million is raised annually by Project Bread's Walk for Hunger in Massachusetts. Over forty thousand men, women, and children participate. To start a walk in your area, call 617-723-5000.

call attention to the hunger problem

Organize events, campaigns, and fundraisers to remind and motivate people to do something about hunger. Pick a local or a national program to benefit; they will be able to supply you with creative ideas.

"By salvaging a precious resource going to waste in our homes, we can help to salvage an even more precious resource going to waste in our streets."

—TEDDY GROSS, *founder*
Common Cents New York
New York City

Share Our Strength's "Taste of the Nation" is a series of food and wine tastings held simultaneously during one week each spring in one hundred cities to raise funds and awareness for groups fighting hunger. More than $4 million have been raised. To participate, call 800-222-1767.

Through Common Cents New York, volunteers harvest their buildings for pennies and donate the money to programs for children and families in need. In one year they collected over $100,000. There are an estimated $1 billion worth of idle pennies in American homes. To set up a harvest in your community, write: Common Cents, 500 Eighth Avenue, New York, NY 10018.

support federal food programs

There are programs in place that if properly implemented can end childhood hunger. One of the most important ones is the Supplemental Food Program to Women, Infants, and Children (WIC), which provides food, nutrition education, and improved access to health care for women and children under five years of age. Currently just over half of those eligible benefit from WIC. Call your local and national politicians. Urge support and implementation of this and other important food programs.

"If we are truly committed to ensuring that no child goes hungry in the United States, we must begin to develop as careful and comprehensive a battle plan for the fight against childhood hunger as we have for political campaigns and military operations."

—Robert J. Fersh, executive director
Food Research and Action Center

The Food Research and Action Center is committed to ending childhood hunger through advocating and organizing local efforts. For advice and information, call 202-986-2200.

In one campaign of Project Bread's "phone tree," calls to politicians resulted in more than $1 million in additional money being appropriated to a federal food program for children.

S T A T I S T I C S

"More children are hungry in the United States than there are total children in such countries as Angola, Somalia, Haiti, Zimbabwe, El Salvador, or Cambodia."
—Children's Defense Fund, *Leave No Child Behind,* p. 42

"Hungry children are two or three times more likely than children from nonhungry families to have suffered from individual health problems, such as frequent colds, unwanted weight loss, fatigue, irritability, headaches, dizziness, and the inability to concentrate."
—The Food Research and Action Center

"Hungry children are absent from school one and a half times as many days as children from nonhungry families."
—The Food Research and Action Center

"Eighty-six percent of the surveyed cities' emergency food assistance facilities must turn away people in need because of lack of resources. Forty-five percent of the cities reported that emergency food assistance facilities are unable to provide adequate quantities of food."
—The United States Conference of Mayors, *A Status Report on Hunger and Homelessness in America's Cities: 1990. 7.*

BREAD FOR THE WORLD
802 Rhode Island Avenue NE
Washington, DC 20018
202-269-0200

CENTER TO PREVENT CHILD-
HOOD MALNUTRITION
3333 K Street, Suite 101
Washington, DC 20007
202-338-6465

THE END HUNGER NET-
WORK
222 North Beverly Drive
Beverly Hills, CA 90210
213-273-3179

FEED THE CHILDREN
Larry Jones International Minis-
tries, Inc.
P.O. Box 36
Oklahoma City, OK 73101
405-942-0228

FOOD INDUSTRY CRUSADE
AGAINST HUNGER
800 Connecticut Avenue NW,
5th Floor
Washington, DC 20006-2701
202-429-4555

FOOD FIRST, INSTITUTE FOR
FOOD AND DEVELOPMENT
POLICY
145 9th Street
San Francisco, CA 94103
415-864-8555 or 800-888-
3314

FOOD RESEARCH AND AC-
TION CENTER
1875 Connecticut Avenue
NW, Suite 540
Washington, DC 20009
202-986-2200

FREEDOM FROM HUNGER
1644 Da Vinci Court
P.O. Box 2000
Davis, CA 95617
916-758-6200

FREESTORE/FOODBANK,
INC.
112 East Liberty Street
Cincinnati, OH 45210
513-241-1064

RESULTS
236 Massachusetts Avenue
NE, Suite 300
Washington, DC 20002
202-543-9340

SAVE THE CHILDREN
54 Wilton Road
Westport, CT 06880
203-221-4000

SECOND HARVEST
National Food Bank Network
116 South Michigan Avenue,
Suite 4
Chicago, IL 60603
312-263-2303

SHARE OUR STRENGTH, INC.
1511 K Street NW, Suite 600
Washington, DC 20005
202-393-2925

U.S.A. HARVEST
P.O. Box 1628
Louisville, KY 40201-1628
800-USA-4-FOOD

C L O T H I N G

"Thank you for the clothes you have given us because if it wasn't for you we would not have any new clothes."
                                —STEPHEN and STEPHANIE
                                 recipients, Back-to-School
                                 Clothes for Kids

"It is not fair that one child can go to school with new, up-to-date clothing . . . and another child starts school in old, worn clothes. . . . I decided to do this work so that life can be just a bit fairer for homeless kids. These children . . . may not have a home, but when it comes to their clothing for the school year, they will be just like the other kids."
                                —CONNIE KENNEDY, founder
                                 Back-to-School Clothes for Kids
                                 White Plains, NY

Many children in this country lack adequate or decent clothing. Their families often cannot cover the cost of buying a winter jacket or a new pair of shoes. It can be crushing for a child always to have to go without or to have less than what other children have. Having proper clothing in good condition can fortify a child's spirits and help build self-esteem. If we all pitched in a little, we could ensure that every child has sufficient clothing—for all seasons.

donate your infants' and other children's clothing

The clothing your children have outgrown could be tremendously helpful to a struggling family. Make a donation directly to a children's organization or a clothing program. Be sure the items are clean and in usable condition. To find out where to bring the clothing, call your local church or synagogue, or ask your volunteer center to suggest a program in need.

"My sister-family is so helpful to me and my children. They always send me things that I can use. My sister-family is also someone I can share my doubt, my fears and my joy with. I have not met my sister-family, only through letters and pictures, but it seems like I really know them. I am eternally grateful."

—GERALDINE O'NEAL *and family*
Box Project members
Plainville, CT

Through the Box Project's Sister Families, a family is connected with a family in need and sends letters monthly, as well as packages of food and clothing. To join their efforts, call 203-747-8182.

i don't have clothes like them

MARIE

Marie, age eight

provide a child with
back-to-school clothes

Many children miss school because they are embarrassed about what they have to wear and fearful of their classmates' making fun of them. Purchase an outfit, or several, for one or more children. Contact a children's program to find out what sizes are needed. Get your friends and coworkers to participate, or ask your company to join in.

"I would like to thank you for buying these clothes for me. It is the first time anyone has given me a variety of clothes to wear to school when I really need it."

—SHAWN, *recipient*
Back-to-School Clothes for Kids
White Plains, NY

In 1986, Connie Kennedy and her friends purchased new school clothing for ten homeless children. In 1991, her organization, Back-to-School Clothes for Kids, provided new school clothing for more than 640 children. To start a similar program in your community, call 914-576-6053.

help a child stay warm in the winter

Having adequate clothing in the cold weather is important not only for a child's health but also for a child's esteem. Save the coats your children have outgrown and any other warm clothing and donate them to a children's program. A coat drive is an excellent project for a group, school, business, or entire community. Publicize your event well, and let people know all the specifics.

"We do everything we can to get the coats off the racks and onto the backs of kids. There is no reason for kids to be cold, especially in this country."

—BILL SEITZ, founder, Coats for Kids
Executive Director, Neighborhood Cleaners Association
New York City

Through Coats for Kids, started by Bill Seitz, executive director of the Neighborhood Cleaners Association, more than fifty thousand coats are cleaned annually at no charge and distributed to children in need throughout New York State. To start a program in your community, call 212-684-0945.

organize a sneaker or a shoe drive

Shoes are expensive and hard to replace for a growing child. Plan a shoe drive and ask people to donate one new pair of shoes, or have a fundraiser and buy new children's shoes with the proceeds. Ask local retailers and manufacturers to contribute. Arrange to make the donations with a children's organization.

"When you see children who are hungry and abused and neglected, who don't have shoes or clothes to wear, how can you turn your back?"

—ESTHER RYAN, founder
Barberton Children's Shoe
Fund
Barberton, OH

doingsomething, a volunteer organization in Washington, DC, held a "shoe-in" in a movie theater and collected fifteen hundred pairs of shoes. Contributors received raffle tickets for prizes donated by local businesses. To hold a similar drive, call 301-891-2468.

Angela, age six

provide new items of clothing

Clothing retailers and manufacturers have excess inventory due to overproduction or slight irregularities. These clothes often needlessly end up as landfill. Retailers and manufacturers can instead donate their unsalable goods to children's organizations and receive tax deductions in return.

"The wonderful thing about a clothing bank is that instead of manufacturers just disposing of excess clothes, they now have a place to send them to where they can benefit the community and reach the people who desperately need them."

—JAMI EDELHEIT, founder
Atlanta Clothing Bank
Network, Inc.
Atlanta, GA

In Atlanta, New York, and San Francisco, clothing banks have been started to distribute brand-new clothing donated from manufacturers to agencies serving individuals and families who are homeless or otherwise in need. To set up a clothing bank in your community, call 404-521-0530.

The Hosiery Industry Cares Foundation connects members of the hosiery industry who have surplus goods with organizations serving individuals and families in need. For information on how and where to donate, call 704-365-0913.

help a child get clothes for camp

A child who gets an opportunity to go to a summer program may not have the clothing needed to do so. Put together a camp package—shorts, T-shirts, bathing suits, underwear, towels, etc. Including toiletry items would be helpful. Your local social service agency or the American Camping Association can link you to a child in need.

"This is the most prettiest dress I've ever seen. I'm going to wear it tomorrow because I'm going on a field trip and I'm going to wear it again everyday."

—EVANGELINA RODRIGUEZ, *eight*
Murphy School District,
Phoenix, AZ

NGA collects and distributes new clothing, linens, and essential toilet articles for individuals and families in need. To find out if there is a branch in your neighborhood or to start one, call 215-322-5759.

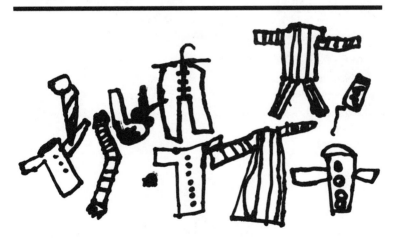

Chris, age six

help a young person get clothes for work

It is difficult for a young person with limited funds to put together a wardrobe for work, or to go on interviews without adequate clothing. Contact a youth organization or community program and offer to purchase or donate appropriate outfits for one or more teens.

Through Dress America, a program started by the National Association of Men's Sportswear Buyers, new clothes are donated to help youths and adults who have been homeless enter the work force. To join their efforts, call 212-391-8580.

THE BOX PROJECT
P.O. Box 435
Plainville, CT 06062
203-747-8182

THE HOSIERY INDUSTRY
 CARES FOUNDATION
c/o National Association of
 Hosiery Manufacturers
447 South Sharon Amity Road
Charlotte, NC 28211
704-365-0913

NGA, INC.
1007-B Street Road
Southhampton, PA 18966
215-322-5759

HOME AND SHELTER

"Children should not have to worry about where we are going to sleep next. We shouldn't worry about when we are going to eat next. Why can't we just be loved and cared for and thought about? That's what we really want."

—BARRY MCKINLAY, *age sixteen*
New York City

"All one has to do is to look into the eyes of homeless children to recognize that, if we are ever going to mend the brokenness of their existence, we must each find a way to touch their lives. We must take advantage of opportunities to connect with them personally, as volunteers, and we must involve ourselves in efforts to change their lives, as advocates."

—FFRED KARNAS, JR., *Ph.D.,*
executive director
National Coalition for the
Homeless

Our home is our foundation. It is the source from which we derive a sense of security and of belonging. Unfortunately, the homes of millions of children in this country are sparse and do not provide even the bare basics. Tens of thousands have no homes and live in shelters, welfare hotels, or on the streets. Others have to be removed from homes that are not physically or emotionally safe, often ending up being shuttled from one place to the next for years to come. While the overall living situation of these children may seem daunting, there are things we all can do right now to help them feel more supported wherever they may be living.

donate your home furnishings

Can you imagine growing up without a table in your kitchen, or without a bed of your own? For millions of American children, that is the reality. Save your household furnishings to donate to families in need. Ask your local retailers and manufacturers to pitch in and contribute new household items. Your local organization for the homeless or housing authority can connect you to a family.

"Children need a decent, safe place to live. It enables them to feel secure from the pressures of the world. It gives them a quiet place to study after school. It provides them a special place where they can be part of a healthy family. We must work to ensure that all children have a home."

—JAMES W. ROUSE, chairman
The Enterprise Foundation
Columbia, MD

To find a coalition for the homeless in your state, check your directory or call the National Coalition for the Homeless at 202-265-2371

Furnish a Future, a program of Partnership for the Homeless, enlists individuals, corporations, hotels, and the furniture and design industry in donating new furnishings. Funds are also raised from the community to purchase household items for newly relocated families. To learn how to set up a similar program, call 718-875-5353.

put together a housewarming package

The needs of a family that has been homeless for any period of time are tremendous. When they finally find permanent housing, it is very difficult to get the resources to set it up properly. They need everything—pots and pans, sheets and towels, light bulbs, brooms, mops. Help one family get started. Ask your volunteer action center about housing programs in your area.

"When I got my new towels and robe, I said, 'Thank the Lord, He answered my prayer.' I wish I could meet the people and thank them."
—Celia, single mother of two
Red Bank, NJ

Dashawn, age six

help transport household items

Often people have furniture or household goods to donate but no means of transporting them. If you have a car or van, offer to pick up and deliver donated items. Ask your local moving companies to pitch in. Your help could mean that available items get to the people who need them.

enhance a small living space

Ask a museum, travel agency, or bookstore to donate posters to brighten up a home. Any decorative items, baskets, or trinkets you have could do a lot to make a home a more welcoming place. Contact a shelter directly or your housing office.

"It's nice that people care about you even though they don't know you. Sometimes you think people don't care, but they must have cared about you to get you that stuff."
—EVELYN, age ten

lend your carpentry or construction skills

Studies show that 22 percent of all Americans who have homes cannot afford to maintain them. As a carpenter, plumber, or electrician, or as a layperson willing to paint, peel, and scrape, you can help a family make their home more livable.

"With hammers and paint brushes we build bridges between people and celebrate our bond as one people."
—PATTY JOHNSON, president
Christmas in April* USA

Habitat for Humanity's Jimmy Carter Work Project brings community members together to build, renovate, and sell homes at no profit to families and individuals in need. For information, call 912-924-6935.

Christmas in April* USA organizes thousands of volunteers across the country to repair and renovate low-income housing. To start a program in your community, call 202-326-8268.

---

help make neighborhoods safe

Drugs and violence have become a way of life in far too many neighborhoods. Help a community band together to reclaim the streets for their children. Participate in or begin a neighborhood safety program.

"Every day, 4,901 teenagers are the victims of violent crimes."
"Every day, 7 teenagers are the victims of homicide."
"Every day, 2 children younger than five are murdered."
                                    —The Children's Defense Fund

---

The National Crime Prevention Council, dedicated to community crime prevention, offers training, materials, and program referrals to set up neighborhood watch programs. For information, call 202-466-6272.

"I'm Safe and Sure" and "I Can Do It" are programs of Camp Fire Girls and Boys designed to teach children personal safety. To get involved, call your local council or 816-756-1950.

doN't take me home those people hate me
                                    Amber, age seven

help out in a shelter

Moving into a shelter can be extremely difficult for a mother and her children. In many cases, this move is a result of a traumatic event—a fire, abuse, or being turned away by family or friends. Contact an organization for the homeless or a church shelter. Spend an evening playing with a child, comforting a mother, serving food, or handing out sheets. A calm and caring presence can be reassuring and helpful to a child suddenly in a strange place.

The Hope Foundation helps meet the needs of shelters nationwide. To find out how you can help a shelter in your area, call 800-843-4073.

---

spend time with children living in a home or a hospital

A consistent relationship with a caring individual can help ease the loneliness, fear, and pain for children living in group homes or hospitals. Your warmth and affection can help a child who has been through trauma and loss begin to trust again, or feel safe. Ask your local hospital or the Department of Child Welfare to refer you to a child in need.

"Babies can withstand almost any kind of suffering, as long as there's someone to love and hold them, to stand between them and their pain."

—GRETCHEN BUCHENHOLZ, *founder*
and executive director
Association to Benefit Children
New York City

advocate for a child in foster care

According to the Child Welfare League of America, there are at least 410,000 children and youth in the foster care system on any given day. Too often, children remain in this overtaxed, understaffed system for months or even years longer than necessary. Become an advocate and represent a child in family court. Speak out to ensure that the child's best interests are met, and that a permanent home is found on a timely basis. Studies show that children who have an advocate spend less time in the system.

"I can think of no more vulnerable population of children than those at risk of removal from the only family they know—abused and neglected children whose cases are before the juvenile court. Lay citizens can make an enormous difference by volunteering as Court-Appointed Special Advocates (CASA) and speaking up for the best interests of these children."

—BETH WAID, executive director
National CASA Association

The goal of Court-Appointed Special Advocates is to match every child in the foster care system with a CASA volunteer by the year 2000. To become an advocate, contact your chapter or call 206-328-8588.

Jaime, age ten

become a foster parent

While every child wants a place where he or she belongs permanently, the need for good foster parents is escalating. According to the National Foster Parent Association, the number of available qualified foster parents is decreasing and has dropped 30 percent since 1984. Open the doors of your home to a child in need. As a certified foster parent you can provide safety and warmth to a child for as little as one weekend, or for years to come.

"Moving from one foster home to another is so hard. I just want to know that I am safe, that I belong somewhere, that someone's going to take care of me."

—MICHAEL, *age nine*

Sheila, age nine

support programs that provide family support and preservation services

According to the Children's Defense Fund, if the trend of children being taken out of their homes continues, by the year 2000 there will be more than half a million children living in the foster care system. Many of these children could remain safely at home if their parents received counseling and support. Urge your politicians to direct money to services designed to preserve the family.

support programs that assist the homeless

Families with children are the fastest-growing segment of the homeless population. According to the National Academy of Sciences, approximately one hundred thousand children sleep on the streets every night. Urge your politicians to support housing assistance and homelessness prevention programs, and to support services to the homeless.

"The plight of homeless children in America, a land of unmatched abundance, must rank as a national tragedy. We know how to solve this problem, and we are compelled, as citizens and as human beings, to do so."

—THOMAS L. KENYON, *president*
National Alliance to End
Homelessness

The National Coalition for the Homeless has a twenty-four-hour hotline to offer suggestions on helping the homeless, as well as information on pending issues and upcoming events. To get involved, call 202-265-2506.

The Homeless Information Exchange is a national information service that provides information on programs and policies on the homeless. For a newsletter or more information, call 202-462-7551.

S T A T I S T I C S

"Parents and their children now make up more than one-third of the total homeless population."

> —Children's Defense Fund, *Leave No Child Behind*, p. 45

"Forty-five hundred dollars spent per family for family preservation can save $10,000 for one year of foster care for one child."

> —Children's Defense Fund

"Seven-hundred sixty-five dollars spent per month for housing assistance, homelessness prevention, and supportive services can save $3,000 just to shelter a homeless family in an inner-city hotel or shelter."

> —Children's Defense Fund

CHRISTMAS IN APRIL* U.S.A.
1225 I Street NW, Suite 601
Washington, DC 20005
202-326-8268

ENTERPRISE FOUNDATION
505 American City Building
Columbia, MD 31044
301-964-1230

HABITAT FOR HUMANITY
121 Habitat Street
Americus, GA 31709-3498
912-924-6935

THE HOPE FOUNDATION
  FOR THE HOMELESS
1555 Regal Row
Dallas, TX 75247
214-630-5765
800-843-4073 (800-THE-
  HOPE)

NATIONAL ALLIANCE TO
  END HOMELESSNESS, INC.
1518 K Street NW, Suite 206
Washington, DC 20005
202-638-1526

NATIONAL ASSOCIATION OF
COMMUNITY ACTION
AGENCIES
1826 18th Street NW, 1st
Floor
Washington, DC 20009
202-265-7546

THE NATIONAL CENTER FOR
NEIGHBORHOOD ENTER-
PRISE
1367 Connecticut Avenue NW
Washington, DC 20036
202-331-1103

THE NATIONAL COALITION
FOR THE HOMELESS
1621 Connecticut Avenue
NW, Suite 400
Washington, DC 20009
202-265-2371

NATIONAL COURT-
APPOINTED SPECIAL ADVO-
CATES
GUARDIAN AD LITEM
2722 Eastlake Avenue E, Suite
220
Seattle, WA 98102
206-328-8588

NATIONAL CRIME PREVEN-
TION COUNCIL
1700 K Street NW, 2nd Floor
Washington, DC 20006
202-466-6272

NATIONAL FOSTER PARENT
ASSOCIATION, INC.
Information and Services Office
226 Kilts Drive
Houston, TX 77024
713-467-1850

ONE ON ONE

SPENDING

TIME

"To feel valued and nurtured can change the course of a life."
—Dr. Michael A. Carrera, director
National Training Center for
Pregnancy Prevention
The Children's Aid Society
New York City

"Children are the future of the world, so if we fail our children then we are, in fact, failing the future of the world we share. A commitment by each citizen to one child would provide the support, motivation, and guidance that we all need to be successful participants in our communities."
—Anthony K. Shriver, president
Best Buddies of America, Inc.
Washington, DC

"One of the most profound effects of poverty and neglect is the intensification of isolation. Likewise, one of the most powerfully healing experiences that we can offer children is our time and our love."
—Dean Ornish, M.D., president
and director
Preventive Medicine Research
Institute
University of California, San
Francisco
San Francisco, CA

FRIENDSHIP
AND SIMPLE PLEASURES

"We've erected a wall of silence around the children of our inner cities. We've stopped listening. We've stopped believing. . . . We must stop to listen, to believe their stories, to respect their yearning to have a childhood . . . filled with innocence and play and hope. We must find ways to break the silence."

—ALEX KOTLOWITZ, *author*
There Are No Children Here

"If just one person had paid me some attention, my life would have been totally different."

—ROBERT, *age eighteen*
prisoner, Rikers Island
New York City

Many children at risk do not have positive role models or sufficient parental guidance. Their parents may be too overwhelmed by the stress and demands of their own lives to have the time or the capacity to listen, pay attention, or encourage their children. For far too many children, some of the basic experiences that we take for granted about childhood are missing. The simple pleasures usually associated with childhood may be unaffordable and out of reach. A relationship with a supportive, constructive individual and provision of positive, childhood experiences can have profound affects, and make all the difference in the direction a child's life takes. These basic elements can help build self-esteem and a sense of hope and possibility. The following are examples of how you can affect a child's life in a direct and personal way.

be a friend to a child

By listening, guiding, and showing an interest, you can help fill in the many gaps in a child's life and make him or her feel lovable, cared for, and worthwhile. You can also be an anchor and offer exposure to the world beyond their immediate environment.

"It's easy to hear all the numbers of children who need help and think it's a hopeless task—that the problem is just too big. But when you volunteer in a school reading program, or as a Big Brother or Big Sister, then you realize that if you help one child, and everyone helps one child, it can make a difference—one child at a time."

—THOMAS M. MCKENNA
national executive director
Big Brothers/Big Sisters of
America

To become a Big Brother or a Big Sister to one of thousands of children waiting, call your local agency or the national office at 215-567-7000.

Kim, age seven

take a child on outings

Bring some joy and excitement into the life of a child. Go to the movies, out for pizza, to the zoo, or bowling. Offer to purchase tickets to a special event such as the circus or a children's play. Many local theaters and sports teams donate blocks of tickets to children's organizations. A local volunteer program or center can help you arrange outings.

"We have to stand behind our young people and give them the support they need today—tomorrow will be too late. It's up to corporations, foundations, and individuals to help provide our country's youth with the leadership and guidance they so desperately need and richly deserve."

—JEREMIAH MILBANK, *chairman*
Boys and Girls Clubs of America

Boys and Girls Clubs of America provide young people with a safe and productive alternative to the streets. To volunteer, call your local club or 212-351-5900.

Marquis, age nine

ask children's museums to open their doors

A children's museum is a great place for a young child to spend time learning, exploring, and creating. Many museums encourage children and families at risk to benefit from their facilities by offering free or discounted admissions, or by offering special classes to mothers and children. Encourage your local museums to reach out in some way.

"Where we come from, the people are nasty and rude and say bad things. At the museum, we're sitting here like normal people in nice surroundings, no yelling or screaming or calling names. It's a different world here. They treat you like a person."

—CONSTANCE FOTOPOULOS
resident, Hotel Regent
participant in the Children's
Museum of Manhattan's
Parent-Child Program New
York City

The Association of Youth Museums can help you identify the youth museums in your area. For information, call 718-273-2493.

The Chicago Children's Museum offers free memberships to all of the families served by forty-seven community service organizations. On their weekly Free Family Night, transportation and snacks are also provided.

help create a safe environment for fun

Playgrounds and parks continually need attention and repair. Many are unsafe. Join in a community effort to clean or maintain the equipment that children use. A once-barren city lot can be transformed into a garden playground with a few packets of seeds and some TLC. If there is no play area in a community, contact the parks and recreation department about creating one.

"An early, positive encounter with nature can be an incredible force in a child's life. Take the children into a forest and let them feel the wonders of this earth, both simple and grand. They will never look at the world or themselves in quite the same way."
—Robert Nixon, producer, *Gorillas in the Mist*
executive director, Earth Conservation Corps

Global Kidz is a unique self-esteem and environmental program for children in which groups work on activities to renew the environment while providing a sense of pride. Their motto says, "The Earth Matters and So Do I." For information about starting your own club, call 404-992-1062.

---

organize a sports activity

Get your friends or coworkers together to play a weekly or monthly game with children from a group home, shelter, or community program. This is a wonderful, relaxed way to get to know some children and for them to get to know you. Bring refreshments along. If funds allow, make up team T-shirts for everyone. A youth center or sporting goods store may lend or donate equipment.

"The main thing I want to accomplish with my program is to give the kids a place to go after school. I want to keep them off the streets. I know I had a chance to play organized baseball, and I want to give today's kids the same chance that I had."
—BOBBY BONILLA, *player*
New York Mets

The Midnight Basketball League, headed by Commissioner Gilbert Walker in Chicago and now operating in seventeen cities, keeps young people off the streets and on the courts. Between 10 P.M. and 2 A.M., young people play basketball and receive job training and counseling between games. To contribute to a program or start one in your area, call 312-791-4768.

Players from the New York Yankees and the New York City Parks Department conduct clinics in various parks to teach children the basics of baseball.

sponsor one child at an enrichment program

What child wouldn't love to learn karate, gymnastics, or dance? A skill like this is something that can set a child apart and make him or her feel special. It can also provide a focus outside of his or her environment. Contact a local after-school program, YMCA, YWCA, or gymnasium and offer to pay for a child who couldn't otherwise afford it. Your donation could be an investment in a child's self-esteem and spark a lifetime of interest.

"Dance has the ability to fill children's lives with the possibility of self-discovery. Young people begin to appreciate their individuality, and how their uniqueness can be positively shared with their peers. The arts can be a conduit that sparks the creative light in every one of us."

> —JUDITH JAMISON, *artistic director*
> *Alvin Ailey American Dance*
> *Theater*

Through YMCA youth programs, young people are provided a wide range of sports, recreation, and developmental activities. To participate, call your local Y.

Mazilas

The cat and dog is going to the Hospital to get Batter.

Fles

Anyon, age thirteen

help send a child to camp

Get your group together to raise the money to send one child to a summer program. There are many that cost very little. Do some research. Check with the Y's in your area. Work with a community program or children's organization to find a likely candidate.

"For inner-city youngsters growing up in tough neighborhoods, childhood can become a period of disillusionment and despair. A volunteer who makes an investment of time, energy, and love by helping one child, definitely makes a difference in the world. We can save the children—one child at a time."

—JENNY MORGENTHAU, *executive director*
The Fresh Air Fund

The Fresh Air Fund provides free summer vacations to children each year. Children visit host families in rural or surburban areas or attend Fresh Air Fund camps. For information on how to sponsor or host a child, call 800-367-0003.

Many sections of the American Camping Association have scholarship funds to send children in need to an accredited camp. See if your local section has a fund.

S   T   A   T   I   S   T   I   C   S

"Approximately one out of every four, or 15 million children in the nation today, is growing up without a father in the home, more than twice as many as 1960."

—Big Brothers/Big Sisters of America

AMERICAN CAMPING ASSO-
  CIATION, NEW YORK SEC-
  TION
12 West 31st Street
New York, NY 10021
212-268-7822

THE ASPIRA ASSOCIATION,
  INC.
1112 16th Street NW, Suite
  340
Washington, DC 20036
202-835-3600

BIG BROTHERS/BIG SISTERS
  OF AMERICA
230 North 13th Street
Philadelphia, PA 19107-1510
215-567-7000

BOYS AND GIRLS CLUBS OF
  AMERICA
771 First Avenue
New York, NY 10017
212-351-5962

CAMP FIRE BOYS AND GIRLS
4601 Madison Avenue
Kansas City, MO 64112
816-756-1950

4-H YOUTH DEVELOPMENT
Extension Service
U.S. Department of Agriculture
1351 Nicholson Avenue NW
Washington, DC 20011
301-961-2800

GIRLS SCOUTS OF THE U.S.A.
830 Third Avenue
New York, NY 10022
212-940-7500

GIRLS, INC.
National Headquarters
30 East 33rd Street
New York, NY 10016
212-689-3700

LIONS CLUBS INTERNA-
  TIONAL
300 22nd Street
Oak Brook, IL 60521-8842
708-571-5466

THE SALVATION ARMY
Director of Volunteers
120 West 14th Street
New York, NY 10011
212-337-7200

VOLUNTEERS OF AMERICA
3813 North Causeway Boulevard
Metairie, LA 70002
504-837-2652

YMCA OF THE U.S.A.
101 North Wacker Drive, 14th
 Floor
Chicago, IL 60606
312-977-0031

YWCA OF THE U.S.A.
726 Broadway
New York, NY 10003
212-614-2700

Dreux, age six

DEVELOPING TALENT

"Well, I've been painting for years . . . ever since I was born, and my latest painting, Tipperty Toes the Elf, is my favorite."
—DAVID, age six
Children of Raphael House,
San Francisco

"The most important thing is to free the imagination of a child because it's limitless and has nothing to do with class, rich, poor, black, or white. The way to improve society is to ensure the future of its artists, and this can only happen by freeing the imagination of the child."
—WENDY WASSERSTEIN, playwright

There is such incredible talent and ability among children. Having a chance to develop these attributes not only brings pleasure but also enhances a child's self-esteem, pride, and sense of feeling capable. Children at risk so rarely experience success or accomplishment. Being encouraged to express themselves and receiving praise and support for doing so can counterbalance much of the negativity they encounter day to day. There are countless ways in which you can help a child develop a talent or an interest. It can be as simple as sharing something you love to do. Here are just a few examples.

teach photography

Taking pictures can be a way for a young person to discover his or her own way of seeing things, to communicate a point of view, and to enjoy. Teach one child or a group of children how to take and develop pictures. Ask a children's organization or your volunteer center to connect you to a program. Try to get film and equipment donated.

"We're all going to have to give something to save the children. They're in a terrible predicament. They're out there with all kinds of temptations. We have to teach them a positive, nonviolent, loving way to deal with this world. We can't leave them alone. They are all our children."

—JIM HUBBARD, *founder*
Shooting Back
Washington, DC

Shooting Back, started by Jim Hubbard, a photojournalist, teaches homeless children how to use a camera. The children's photos have appeared in *Life* magazine and have toured the country. To find out more, write Shooting Back, 1901 18th Street NW, Washington, DC 20009.

José Loís, age eight

teach an art class

If you enjoy arts and crafts and have some background, contact a youth program or children's organization and offer to lead a class in art. Painting, making collages, sculpting, and drawing are great creative outlets for children. Programs often lack the funds to hire a teacher, so your participation may make a class possible.

"If we just help the children on our own block or in our own apartment building we can make a huge difference. If we do not teach these children something constructive to do, they will teach our children something destructive."

—Delores Beall, S.W.,
founder/executive director
I Am That I Am Training Center
Dallas, TX

After seeing youths vandalizing cars in her church's parking lot, Delores Beall founded I Am That I Am Training Center in Dallas, TX, to provide arts programs, tutoring, and friendship to children and youths in need of attention and direction.

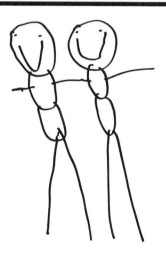

Adam, age five

offer to show children's artwork

It can be an unforgettable moment in a child's life to have his or her artwork exhibited. Contact a local children's arts program and offer to sponsor an art show in the lobby of your office building, at your place of worship, or at your club. Have an opening party and invite the press, members of the community, and the artists and their families. The impact can be very positive for everyone involved.

"It must be conveyed to children, especially those who are poor or are members of a minority group, that they have been endowed with a wealth of talent and that in the end, talent and tenacity, not money, determine whether they will become successful in life."

—*GEORGE E. CURRY, director*
New York Minority Journalism
Workshop
N.Y. Bureau Chief
The Chicago Tribune

Laura, age seven

start a community arts program

Get a group of children together and create a community project. Painting a mural, for example, is a wonderful group experience and can enhance a dreary neighborhood. It can give children a great sense of accomplishment to be able to leave their mark, in a positive way, on their community. Get permission from the proper city group to execute the project, and contact a local artist to help with the design.

"The arts can be an important way to achieve a sense of accomplishment that might otherwise be lacking. A child can struggle with math or reading, but the joy and pride that is realized by creating a painting, piece of sculpture or a dance is incredible and can have a positive effect on other areas of a child's life."
—BETH RUDIN DEWOODY, *director*
Samuel and May Rudin
Foundation

Brookie Maxwell, a sculptor and painter, founded Creative Arts for Children Workshops. With the help of volunteers and donated cans of paint, children create colorful murals and sculptures and bring hopes and dreams to Harlem streets.

Laura Kate, age six

offer scholarships

Arts programs, Y's, and community centers can offer scholarships for children and youth at risk to participate in their after-school or weekend programs. It is so important for children to have constructive experiences and to expand their horizons. Ask your community center or the program your child attends to consider opening its doors to a child in need.

"We're blessed to be able to share and blessings are for sharing."
—ANNA STRASBERG, *cofounder and
artistic director
The Lee Strasberg Theatre
Institute
New York City*

The Lee Strasberg Theatre Institute in New York City, Los Angeles, and London offers scholarships to children at risk on a regular basis. Children and teens learn method acting in the classrooms where Marilyn Monroe and James Dean once studied.

Through Young Aspiration/Young Artists, Inc., high school students in New Orleans are given free art training as well as the proceeds from the sale of their work, a percentage of which goes into a college trust fund.

OPENING DOORS

CREATING

OPPORTUNITIES

"Everyone, irrespective of age, profession, background, or circumstances, has a gift to give—from corporate employees to the neighborhood bowling club. By giving unconditionally of our time, talent, and resources, we can offer a better future for our children and add meaning and adventure to our own lives as well."
— C. GREGG PETERSMEYER, assistant
to the President and director,
Office of National Service
The White House

"Maybe you can't save all the world's children. But maybe you don't have to. Maybe if you make life a little better for one group, with one problem, or even make things better for just one child, that's enough."
— KERRY KENNEDY CUOMO, executive
director
Robert K. Kennedy Memorial
Center for Human Rights
New York City

"The conditions and problems faced by our children seem so intrinsic and unsolvable that people become numb and paralyzed. I encourage each person to view every child as full of potential requiring guidance, protection, and resources. I encourage every adult to become involved in some way that helps a child realize that potential."
— SHARON JOHNSON, executive
director
Northside Center for Child
Development
New York City

E D U C A T I O N

"Usually child abuse is described in terms of flagrant physical and/or psychological rejection of defenseless children. The more subtle and prevalent form is the abusing of children who attend schools and leave without an adequate education."

> —KENNETH B. CLARK *distinguished professor emeritus City University of New York author,* Prejudice and Your Child, Dark Ghetto

One of four students does not complete high school. One of four thirteen-year-olds cannot add, subtract, or multiply and divide using whole numbers. One of eight seventeen-year-olds is functionally illiterate, which means his or her reading and writing skills are below sixth-grade level. These alarming statistics are a cause for great concern. Without a strong academic foundation, our children's chance for independent living and ability to operate in the work force is severely hindered. An investment of time to support and encourage young people academically, as well as to fight for quality schools for all children, will ultimately serve not only our children but also our nation. This chapter offers suggestions on how we can all get involved.

help out in a preschool program

Studies demonstrate that children who have participated in preschool programs show dramatic improvements in both academic and social skills and competency. Support your community's efforts to provide early childhood education. Volunteer your time, donate supplies, or make a financial contribution. Call your local school or school district for help locating a program.

"Children that I have worked with appeared to be slow learners. Therefore, they were considered to be at risk. However, all they needed was a helping hand and they took off like rockets in the sky."
—CRISTELA ROCHA, student
St. Edward's University
Austin, TX

A nineteen-year study of one hundred at-risk youth who had attended the High/Scope Perry Preschool Program in Ypsilanti, MI, showed a 50 percent increase in college attendance and employment and dramatic decreases in teen pregnancy, arrests, and dropouts. The High/Scope curriculum developed during this study is now widely used.

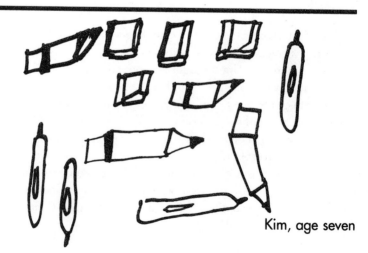

Kim, age seven

become a mentor

Studies of students who have mentors show dramatic increases in school performances. In a Louis Harris poll of four hundred high school juniors and seniors who had mentors, 87 percent went directly to college or planned to attend within one year of graduating. As a mentor you have the opportunity to provide a child or young person with a positive role model. You can offer the support and encouragement often lacking in their lives. Your concern and attention can help a young person recognize his or her potential and set positive goals.

"Too many children today are living in poverty and dysfunctional families, vulnerable to substance abuse and teenage pregnancy. These children are at risk of dropping out of school for lack of hope, encouragement, and positive alternatives. You can be a mentor for a child—a positive role model. A little of your time can last a lifetime for a child."

—Matilda Cuomo, First Lady of
New York State
Founder, New York State
Mentoring Program

Help One Student to Succeed operates mentoring programs that teach children reading, writing, vocabulary, and life and study skills. To become involved in one of four hundred programs nationwide, call 800-833-4678.

The National Media Outreach Center has nearly five hundred contacts for mentoring programs nationwide. To be referred to a program in your area, call their Plus Project at 412-622-1491.

help a child with homework

Many parents are unable or unavailable to help children with their schoolwork. Many homes are not conducive to the concentration needed to complete homework assignments. Help a child build study habits and strengthen academic skills by volunteering in an after-school homework help program. Your presence can build confidence and help a child feel comfortable enough to ask for the help he or she may be too embarrassed to ask for in school. Ask your local volunteer center to recommend a program. If your community doesn't have one, contact a school principal to see if you and your group can get one started.

"I love my tutor. She talks to me about my problems like when I thought I was ugly because I didn't have braces. She helps me with my school work and how I feel about me."

—Nena Graham, age ten
Rainbow Achievement Program
Billingsville Elementary School

The Citizens Committee for New York City has pamphlets on how to start a homework help program in your neighborhood. To order a pamphlet, call 212-684-6767.

I learned how to speak Corret English.

say dog what up

how are you doing today

Denise, age eight

volunteer in a dropout prevention program

According to the National Collaboration for Youth, about one million young people drop out of school each year. Each year's class of dropouts will eventually cost approximately $240 billion in lost earnings and taxes. There are programs designed to lower the dropout rate by building both academic skills and self-esteem and by providing students the encouragement and incentives to complete school.

"My mentor is the best friend I ever had."
—STEPHANIE CALDERAN, *fifth-grader*
Project Mentor, Austin, TX

Cities In Schools, Inc., provides counseling and a wide range of social services right on the premises of a school to reach students and to discourage dropping out. To volunteer in a program in your area or to start one in a local school, call 703-519-8999.

In 1990, at Harding High School in Bridgeport, CT 120 ninth-graders, thirty volunteers, and many teachers worked together to lower the dropout rate. Through seminars, workshops, and general support they lowered the dropout rate from 30 percent in 1989 to 16 percent in 1990, a reduction of 47 percent. The National Dropout Prevention Center can link you with a program for at-risk youth in your area. For information, call 803-656-2599.

help children get school supplies

Millions of children cannot afford the basics needed to do their schoolwork. Put together a back-to-school package for one or more children. Include pens, pencils, notebooks, paper, a dictionary, a ruler, etc. Organize a group of friends, coworkers, or classmates to join you. A social service agency or volunteer center can help to set this up, or you can call a shelter directly.

"Even after sixteen years of bringing awareness of this need, I am amazed that most Americans don't realize the plight of poor children in schools; for the children school supplies are 'tools of life' because education is their only way out of poverty."
—Nick Monreal, Jr.,
director/founder
Teach the Children
San Antonio, TX

Teach the Children in San Antonio, TX, was founded by Nick Monreal, Jr., after he saw a student use a crumpled piece of paper from a garbage can for schoolwork. Today, thousands of children receive school supplies from chapters across the country. To start one in your community, call 512-680-0217.

---

help a parent help a child

Many parents feel they cannot help their children because they themselves lack academic skills. Join a support group for parents and convey to them that their involvement and interest in their children's education can be more important than their understanding of the subject matter. Encourage parents to become active in the schools and to meet with their children's teachers. Your local PTA can be helpful in arranging this.

"One-on-one communication is very important. It communicates to a child that he counts, that he is important. It helps build self-esteem, and that is everything."

—Susan Edgar, executive director
New York School Volunteer
Program

Through Adopt a Family for Educational Excellence Project in Montgomery, AL, college students and adult volunteers go into the homes of high-risk students and help the parents get involved in their children's academic development. For information on how to set up a similar program, call 205-240-6900.

Michael, age twelve

support scholarship funds for high school students

There are programs that give motivated students from low-income backgrounds the opportunity to attend a school that can provide an academic challenge. These programs also offer mentoring to participants to ensure academic success and to guide them toward a college education. Support one of these programs by making a financial contribution or by becoming a mentor.

"The future of our society depends on children who believe in the beauty, glory, and imagination of their dreams. We must all encourage our children to dream and help them to believe."

> —EUGENE LANG, *founder and chairman*
> *"I Have a Dream" Foundation*
> *New York City*

A Better Chance selects academically talented minority students nationwide and facilitates their access to career information and educational enrichment options, including the opportunity for placement at one of 160 college preparatory schools. For information, call 617-421-0950.

The "I Have a Dream" Foundation offers long-term support and guidance for college prep or job placement to thousands of at-risk students nationwide. To offer sponsorship and support, contact your local chapter or call 212-736-1730.

---

fight for school reforms

Investments in our schools now can help children realize their potential as well as save our nation billions of dollars. Call your local community board, PTA, or advocacy group to see what you can do to ensure that all children get the education they deserve.

"If we truly believe that our children are our most important resource, then we must nurture them. Education is the ticket to their future. A quality education is every child's fundamental and natural right and is the key to a thriving, prosperous, and democratic society."
—CAROLE ISENBERG, and LYNDA
GUBER, cofounders
Education First!
Los Angeles

America 2000 is a nationwide campaign of the U.S. Department of Education to enhance the quality and level of education in America by the year 2000. To find out how you or your organization can help, call your governor's office or 800-USA-LEARN.

Adam, age five

support federally funded early childhood education programs

Founded in 1965, Head Start, the largest federally funded early childhood program, has overwhelmingly proven the significance of early childhood education. Studies show that children who participate are more likely to graduate from school and get a job, and are less likely to have an early pregnancy or get arrested. Yet only one of four children who are eligible are able to attend due to lack of funding. Call your politicians. Urge them to support allotment of funds to and implementation of Head Start and other preschool programs. An investment in these programs now can save billions of dollars in later remedial costs.

"The single most effective and efficient interaction on behalf of children is a comprehensive and well-coordinated early childhood program . . . to ensure that every child arrives at kindergarten physically, mentally, emotionally, and socially ready to succeed in the world of learning."

—R. H. WEHLING, vice president,
public affairs
The Procter & Gamble
Company
Cincinnati, OH

A BETTER CHANCE, INC.
419 Boylston Street
Boston, MA 02116
617-421-0950

AMERICA 2000
U.S. Department of Education
Washington, DC 20202-0498
800-USA-LEARN

CITIES IN SCHOOLS, INC.
401 Wythe Street, Suite 200
Alexandria, VA 22314-1963
703-519-8999

HEAD START
U.S. Department of Health and
  Human Services
Head Start Bureau
P.O. Box 1182
Washington, DC 20213
202 245-0572

HELP ONE STUDENT TO SUC-
  CEED (HOSTS)
1801 D Street
Vancouver, WA 98663-3332
800-833-4678

"I HAVE A DREAM" FOUNDA-
TION
330 Seventh Avenue
New York, NY 10001
212-736-1730

NATIONAL ASSOCIATION
FOR THE ADVANCEMENT
OF COLORED PEOPLE
(NAACP)
4805 Mount Hope Drive
Baltimore, MD 21215
410-486-9149

NATIONAL COLLABORATION
OF YOUTH
1319 F Street NW, Suite 601
Washington, DC 20004
202-347-2080

NATIONAL COMMITTEE FOR
CITIZENS IN EDUCATION
900 2nd Street, NE, Suite 8
Washington, DC 20002-3557
202-408-0447

NATIONAL COUNCIL OF NE-
GRO WOMEN, INC.
(PROJECT REACH)
P.O. Box 337
Central Islip, NY 11722
516-234-9060

THE NATIONAL DROPOUT
PREVENTION CENTER
205 Martin Street
Clemson University
Clemson, SC 29634-5111
803-656-2599

THE NATIONAL MEDIA OUT-
REACH CENTER
The Plus Project on Mentoring
4802 Fifth Avenue
Pittsburgh, PA 15213
412-622-1491

THE NATIONAL PARENT
TEACHER ASSOCIATION
700 North Rush Street
Chicago, IL 60611-2571
312-787-0977

NATIONAL URBAN LEAGUE
The Equal Urban Opportunity
Building
500 East 62nd Street
New York, NY 10021
212-310-9000

UNCOMMON INDIVIDUAL
FOUNDATION
2 Radnor Station, Suite 214
290 King of Prussia Road
Radnor, PA 19087
215-964-1642

UNITED NEGRO COLLEGE
FUND
500 East 62nd Street
New York, NY 10021
212-326-1236

L I T E R A C Y

"I think the tutors should stay, because they help us in social studies, Math, English, science, wrighting, and all that stuff."
>—STEPHANIE ALVAREZ, *age ten*
>Travis Heights Elementary
>School
>Austin, TX

"We all know that helping children get started well is perhaps the most important thing in which any of us could invest our time, talents, commitment and resources."
>—MARGOT WODELL, *project director*
>PBS Project Education
>general manager, WQED
>Pittsburgh, PA

Millions of children grow up in illiterate households. They do not receive the support they need to excel in school, which results in their starting off far behind their peers. Without basic skills a child's chances for future independence, productivity, and success are greatly limited. According to Project Literacy U.S., children with low basic skills are nine times more likely to drop out of high school, eight times more likely to become pregnant out of wedlock, and four times more likely to become welfare-dependent than children with above-average skills. This chapter offers suggestions on how we can break the cycle of illiteracy and guide our children into brighter futures.

donate children's books

Save your children's books and donate them to a shelter or community center. Ask your local bookstores to pitch in. It is essential for children to be exposed to books at a young age; yet many children grow up having none.

"Children are our most precious resource. Each of us can help today's children to grow up prepared for a bright future. OUR volunteers nationwide are helping by opening young minds to learning and to the world of imagination and adventure that lie between the covers of books."

—ANNE RICHARDSON, chairman of the board
Reading Is Fundamental, Inc.
(RIF)

Reading Buddies, a collaborative project of RIF Nabisco Biscuit Co., and MCA/Universal Studios encourages children to read. For more information, call 202-287-3220.

Barnes & Noble runs a Children's Holiday Book Drive in some of its stores. They set up bins, ask customers to contribute new books, and match each purchase. In the first year, six thousand books were collected. In the second year, twenty-eight thousand were collected and distributed throughout New York City.

---

get your organization to sponsor a book drive

Large numbers of books can be gathered and donated through collective efforts. Suggest a drive to your coworkers or group members. Many publishers are already involved in children's literacy efforts and may be able to contribute to your drive. Link up with a literacy program to distribute books, or donate them to a local children's organization or community center directly.

". . . one of our primary motivations as publishers is not only getting our children to read but to show them that reading is fun! . . . We'd like to make a small contribution to helping to make a positive difference in the lives of the kids . . . in our corporate hometown."

—JACK HOEFT, president and chief executive officer Bantam Doubleday Dell Publishing Group

---

United Way of America's publication *Achieving National Literacy by the Year 2010: A Call to Action* outlines a role for every institution, business, and organization to help prevent and remedy illiteracy. To find out what you can do, call your local United Way.

As part of Bantam Doubleday Dell's (BDD) adoption of five first-grade classes in New York City schools, employees organize and lead parent, teacher, and student activities. BDD also donates a thousand books per school and arranges visits from authors and illustrators.

The Books for Kids Foundation has placed half a million books in the hands of children in need through the contributions of publishing companies. To make a donation, call 212-472-0864.

---

help a parent learn to read

A parent who can read is better equipped to help a child develop academically. Help break the cycle of illiteracy. Join a literacy program. Just an hour of your time a week can strengthen children and their families.

The National Literacy Hotline can locate a literacy project in your area. To find one, call 800-228-8813.

RIF's Project Open Book sets up reading centers for children in community centers and welfare hotels. To date publishers and distributors have donated more than 800,000 books, which the children are welcome to keep. For more information,call 202-287-3220.

Dashawn, age six

start a reading circle for parents and children

Studies show the importance of children being read to at an early age in terms of developing reading and language skills. Yet many young parents lack the precedent of story time. Offer to lead a group of parents in reading to their children. Set this up through a literacy group, or ask a library to host a program. Gather books from donations, or hold a drive so that both parents and children can take books home with them.

"Whatever you can do to uplift the life of a child, be it your own or someone else's, is a step in the right direction toward creating true civil rights for children. I believe in the philosophy of each one, teach one. If you don't have children, find someone else's! Take them to the library, the theater, a picnic in the park. Use your own life to help point a young life in the right direction."
—OPRAH WINFREY

Shared Beginnings, a RIF program, is designed to empower teen parents to create a legacy of reading and learning for their young families. To get involved, call 202-287-3220.

link children with libraries

Libraries are accessible and free, and in most cases have a special awareness of the needs of children. Help children from a shelter, school, or community program become familiar with their library. Not only are libraries helpful with reading, they are also a safe and supportive place for children to develop study habits.

"Reading is like the base of a pyramid. If I can help a child by listening to them read, as a team we could build a strong foundation for future growth and understanding."
—KATHY MCALISTER
Adopt-a-School
Fort Worth, TX

To celebrate reading, the Bruce-Monroe Elementary School in Washington, DC, held a slumber party. Students, business leaders, politicians, the school's staff, and media personalities read until the children fell asleep.

S T A T I S T I C S

"As many as twenty-three million adult Americans are functionally illiterate, lacking basic skills beyond a fourth-grade level. Another thirty-five million are semiliterate, lacking skills beyond an eighth-grade level.

"The United States Department of Labor estimates that adult illiteracy costs society an estimated $225 billion annually in lost productivity, unrealized tax revenue, welfare, crime, poverty, and related social ills."
—PROJECT LITERACY U.S.

ACHIEVING NATIONAL LITER-
ACY BY THE YEAR 2010—A
CALL TO ACTION
United Way of America
701 North Fairfax Street
Alexandria, VA 22314
703-836-7100

THE BARBARA BUSH FOUN-
DATION FOR FAMILY LITER-
ACY
1002 Wisconsin Avenue NW
Washington, DC 20007
202-338-2006

LITERACY VOLUNTEERS OF
AMERICA, INC.
5795 Widewaters Parkway
Syracuse, NY 13214-1846
315-445-8000 or 800-228-
8813 (Contact Literacy Hotline)

PROJECT LITERACY U.S.
The National Media Outreach
Center
4802 Fifth Avenue
Pittsburgh, PA 15213
412-622-1491

READING IS FUNDAMENTAL,
INC.
Smithsonian Institution
600 Maryland Avenue, SW,
Suite 500
Washington, DC 20024
202-287-3220

TIME TO READ
Time Warner, Inc.
1271 Avenue of the Americas
New York, NY 10020
212-522-1212

Kings County Hospital.

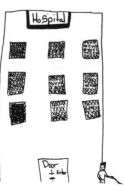

Marquis, age nine

WHAT BUSINESSES CAN DO

"For our sake, we need to invest in the children of poverty. If we make the investment during their first years—from prenatal care through the age of four—those children can succeed. We will get our investment back plus interest, plus inflation, plus a 300 percent to 500 percent profit. This is not a guess, it is proved by research. There is not a more profitable investment that we can make."

> —BRAD BUTLER, chairman
> Committee for Economic
> Development

"In a completely rational society, the best of us would be teachers, and the rest of us would be something less."

> —LEE IACOCCA, chairman of the
> Board and CEO,
> Chrysler Corporation

During the past decade there has been a growing movement by businesses to participate in efforts to improve children's chances for success. Fueled by the understanding that the quality of education will directly affect our nation's future work force, more than two hundred thousand businesses across the nation have committed to ensuring that young people get the support they need to stay in school and are prepared to meet the growing demands of the work force upon graduating. Following are suggestions on how you and your business can join in.

encourage employees to volunteer

Businesses can list volunteer opportunities in newsletters or memos. If you are involved in a program and would like to interest others, ask for information to be listed in your company's publication. Some companies give employees release time for community projects as well as match employee volunteer hours with contributions.

"I think my mentor is a very intelligent lady, I feel as I can tell her anything that's on my mind, and she'd understand. I think more mentors should come to Mendez Middle School."

—DOROTHY ANN TREVINO, *age fifteen*
Project Mentor
Austin, TX

Federal Express Corporation allows release time for its employees to help high school students in Memphis, Tennessee explore career, vocational and personal goals.

Augusto, age seven

start a mentoring program

A business is an ideal place for starting a mentoring program. It can be done at the office, a school, or a community center. If your company has a program, join in. If it doesn't, find out about setting one up. Seeing a young person begin to change his or her attitudes about life and its possibilities through your support and encouragement can be as rewarding to you as it is to a youth.

"Let us not forget that every child needs an advocate, an adult who takes time to share and to love. Volunteers are the advocates for America's schoolchildren."

—DAN MERENDA, *executive director*
National Association of
Partners in Education

As a result of the Norwalk Mentor Program in Connecticut, which matches volunteers from the business community with children of kindergarten age and up, 90 percent of the students increased their reading and spelling skills or interests, 87 percent improved school attendance, and 92 percent increased their self-confidence.

Through Mentors, Inc., in Washington, DC, mentors are recruited from corporations, government agencies, universities, and professional firms. Their goal is to provide each young person in the District of Columbia area with a mentor throughout high school. For help doing the same for your community's children, call 202-393-0512.

The National One to One Partnership Kit guides businesses in establishing mentoring programs. To order, call 202-338-3844.

donate supplies and equipment

Your company can help a school or youth program get much-needed and often unaffordable items and at the same time receive a tax deduction. If you are moving or have excess supplies, inventory, or office equipment, make a donation to a school or program in need.

Ralston Purina provides classroom space and office equipment to a business education program for high school seniors from St. Louis schools.

The National Association for the Exchange of Industrial Resources channels $75 million of excess inventory each year from businesses to schools and nonprofit organizations. To get your business involved, call 800-562-0955.

Tiara, age six

WHAT BUSINESSES CAN DO   103

provide training to teachers

Help teachers enable their students to be better prepared for the world of work by providing seminars on the latest advancements and opportunities in your field. Keep teachers up to date on current technologies and trends.

"One of the primary strengths of the American people lies in their ability to join together in associations to achieve what no one person could achieve alone. Associations all over this country realize the importance of investing time in helping children and are actively involved in activities such as adopt-a-school, mentoring, and scholarship programs. These children are our futures, but they need our help now."

—R. WILLIAM TAYLOR, CAE,
president
American Society of
Association Executives

The Committee for Economic Development helps businesses identify problems and focus on solutions through partnerships with education and the community. To find out more information, call 212-688-2063.

The Boeing Company invites the office staff of its partnered school in Seattle, Washington to attend training seminars.

form a partnership with a school

There is a strong and growing trend of businesses to enter into partnerships with schools to help them meet the challenge of providing quality education to its students. By working in conjunction with the school principal, your business can analyze the needs of the school and decide how best to utilize your expertise and resources to meet these needs. From offering managerial skills to developing vocational training programs, your business can help a school meet the challenge of educating its students and in turn impact the readiness of its students for the work force.

"It is not enough to extol the virtues of volunteerism. We must also build sturdy mechanisms that enable people to really help."
> —Marc Freedman, *director of special projects Public/Private Ventures author,* The Kindness of Strangers: Reflections on the Mentoring Movement

The National Association of Partners in Education assists schools, businesses, and communities throughout the country in setting up partnerships. For information, call 703-836-4880.

The Principal for a Day program of the Los Angeles Educational Partnership Program and the Los Angeles School District brings CEOs from companies such as Arco, IBM, GTE, and Rockwell International to a day in a principal's office to learn about school life from firsthand experience.

teach job-readiness skills

Youth at risk need preparation for and encouragement about entering the workplace. You can help. Share tips on interviewing, what to wear, and office etiquette. Help write a résumé, or assist in filling out job applications. Your support and guidance can give much-needed confidence. Contact a school directly, or ask a national business organization to link you to a group in need.

"If there's one thing I've learned, it's this: Programs don't change kids, relationships do. Nothing matters more to a child than a one-to-one, steady relationship with an adult who cares about that child."
—BILL MILLIKEN, *president*
Cities In Schools, Inc.

The Private Industry Council provides job training to young people at risk and arranges for employers to hire these youths. To offer positions, call your local chapter or 202-289-2950.

Public/Private Ventures works with schools, businesses, and government to improve youth's preparation. For information, call 215-592-9099.

Rockwell International supports more than 200 education-related programs throughout the U.S. They provide financial contributions, teacher enhancement, educational support and personal involvement of their employees.

teach your trade

Share what you do with a young person. Learning a trade, a skill, or how to operate a business offers not only practical information but also gives a sense of guidance and a connection to the working community.

"The gap is so tremendous between mentor and protégé that I feel if the only accomplishment is to show a student a different side of life—if only for a few hours a month—it may open his or her eyes to a dream, something different to strive for and aspire to."
                    —MONA WEISBERG, real-estate
                    consultant
                    Philadelphia Futures
                    Philadelphia, PA

Junior Achievement, Inc., helps businesses around the world prepare the future work force through economic education. For information, call 719-540-8000.

Boys and Girls Clubs of America's One-with-One career exploration program provides career guidance to youth by matching them with adult mentors. To volunteer, call your local chapter or 212-351-5900.

---

make a presentation about your career

Arrange with a school or community center to visit and speak with the young people about your career. Invite friends or colleagues from different fields to join you. This can be done as a series of informal talks or as a job fair.

"Everyone in the business community has something to offer to enhance the life of a child at risk. Giving something of ourselves and sharing our resources can put our children on the right path. The rewards of giving will benefit us all."

—MICHAEL STERN, president
French Impressions
Founder, the Graduate
Achievement Program
New York City

Through A Day in the Life, entrepreneurs Michael and Marjorie Stern encourage members of the community to inspire young people toward achievement by sharing knowledge and experience.

Allison, age six

offer job exposure

The more information and exposure young people have to the work world, the more inspired and informed their decisions about their futures can be. Invite a group from a school or youth program to visit you at work. Talk about general job decorum, entry-level positions, salaries, and job requirements.

"As a nation, we know a lot more about what children need to become healthy adults than we ever put to use. It would be a sad testimony, indeed, to say we passed through our lives and did less than we could to help our children."
                    —*NORMAN BROWN, president*
                    W. K. Kellogg Foundation
                    Battle Creek, MI

Through the Boston Private Industry Council, over 350 businesses give priority hiring to Boston public-school graduates. To find out more, call 617-423-3755.

Career Beginnings helps youth at risk gain the skills and the credentials they need to enter college, training programs, or the work force by matching students with mentors from the business community. To become a workplace partner, call 617-736-4990.

offer an internship in your office or business

No matter how simple a task, you can benefit from getting a job done and give a young person the chance to get his or her feet wet in a business environment. An internship is an excellent way for a young person to learn about the world of work in a supportive situation. Ask your friends or colleagues to offer positions as well.

The Executive Internship Program helps students learn by doing by placing more than a thousand students a year with successful businessmen and professionals. To set up a similar program, call 212-741-1152.

---

offer a summer job

Identify a position in your company that would be appropriate for a young person. Contact the job counselor at a community program or high school to find an appropriate candidate. Assign one employee as a guide or mentor. A summer job is a good introduction and preparation—and can help a youth gain some much-needed income.

"America is failing its youth. It is accepting attitudes, behavior, social mores, and outcomes that will lead to economic disaster. We can no longer pretend the problem does not exist or is not a factor in our competitiveness."

—WILLIAM H. KOLBERG, president
National Alliance of Business
Washington, D.C.

More than ninety-three hundred high-school students have benefited from the IBM Summer Youth Work/Study Program, which combines summer jobs with training to improve academic and job-preparation skills.

donate a percentage of the sale of a product or service

Businesses are becoming aware of the public-relations potential in philanthropy. There is a growing trend for companies, products, and services to be associated with an organization or a cause. Find a way for your company to participate. The benefits are mutual.

"Today's children are tomorrow's most precious resource. We must take the time to inspire, to motivate, and to encourage our children. We need to help them set goals for themselves, and to stand beside them willingly of ourselves as they seek to realize those goals."
—FRANK V. CAHOUET, *president, chairman, and CEO*
Mellon Bank Corporation
Pittsburgh, PA

The Wise Giving Guide and *Before You Give* are two booklets published by the National Charities Information Bureau to help people make informed financial contributions. To order copies, call 212-929-6300.

Over the past five years, Mellon Bank Corporation has contributed in cash, in-kind donations, and volunteer time more than $59 million to charitable organizations.

strengthen families

Your business can help both young parents and their children. You can offer day care, parental leave, health insurance for both parents and children, and education. An investment in the parents can ensure children's healthy development and future productivity.

Honeywell, Inc. sponsors Phillip's Tender Loving Care, a community-wide effort to ensure that young pregnant mothers receive proper prenatal care. The goal is to reduce infant mortality and the number of low birthweight babies.

ASSOCIATION OF SCHOOL/ BUSINESS PARTNERSHIP DI- RECTORS
c/o Norwalk Public Schools
125 East Avenue
P.O. Box 6001
Norwalk, CT 06852-6001
203-854-4011

CAREER BEGINNINGS PRO- GRAM
Heller Graduate School
Brandeis University
60 Turner Street
Waltham, MA 02254-9110
800-343-4705
617-736-4990

COMMITTEE FOR ECO- NOMIC DEVELOPMENT
477 Madison Avenue
New York, NY 10022
212-688-2063

COUNCIL FOR AID TO EDU- CATION
51 Madison Avenue, Suite 2200
New York, NY 10010
212-689-2400

GOODWILL INDUSTRIES OF AMERICA
9200 Wisconsin Avenue
Bethesda, MD 20814
301-530-6500

JUNIOR ACHIEVEMENT, INC.
45 East Clubhouse Drive
Colorado Springs, CO 80906
719-540-8000

MANPOWER DEVELOPMENT
  CORPORATION
1717 Legion Road
Chapel Hill, NC 27514
919-968-4531

NATIONAL ACADEMY FOUN-
  DATION
31 W 52nd Street, 9th Floor
New York, NY 10019

NATIONAL ALLIANCE OF
  BUSINESS
1201 New York Avenue NW,
  Suite 700
Washington, DC 20005
202-289-2888

NATIONAL ASSOCIATION OF
  BLACK JOURNALISTS
Mentor/Protege Program
P.O. Box 17212
Washington, DC 20041
703-648-1270

NATIONAL ASSOCIATION
  FOR THE EXCHANGE OF
  INDUSTRIAL RESOURCES
560 McClure Street
P.O. Box 8076
Galesburg, IL 61402
309-343-0704

NATIONAL ASSOCIATION OF
  PARTNERS IN EDUCATION,
  INC.
209 Madison Street, Suite 401
Alexandria, VA 22314
703-836-4880

ONE TO ONE
2801 M Street NW
Washington, DC 20007
202-338-3844

PRIVATE INDUSTRY COUNCIL
17 Battery Place, 5th Floor
New York, NY 10004
212-742-1000

PUBLIC/PRIVATE VENTURES
399 Market Street
Philadelphia, PA 19106
215-592-9099

ROTARY INTERNATIONAL
1560 Sherman Avenue
Evanston, IL 60201
708-866-3000

HEALTHY
BEGINNINGS
STRONG STARTS

"It lies within our reach, before the end of the twentieth century, dramatically to improve the early lives of several million American children growing up at grave risk. We can substantially improve the odds that they will become healthy, sturdy, and productive adults, participants in a twenty-first-century America whose aspirations they will share. The cycle of disadvantage that has seemed so intractable can be broken."

—LISBETH B. SCHORR
member of the Harvard
University Working Group on
Early Life
author of Within Our Reach:
Breaking the Cycle of
Disadvantage

"I firmly believe that we must create a safe, loving, and healthy environment for children to grow up in. As we rush headlong toward the turn of the millennium, there is no more important an endeavor than that of nurturing the hearts and minds of our children. It is imperative that we as adults take personal responsibility for manifesting this ideal."

—LEVAR BURTON, actor

"The cost of reaching our children at risk may be daunting, but the cost of failing to reach these children is more than our society can possibly afford."

—ROGER WEISBERG, producer,
director
PBS documentary Our Children
at Risk

HEALTH AND INFANT MORTALITY

"It's scary when you're sick and your mom can't take you to the doctor."

—Tito, *age eight, New York City*

"Unless we act today, in the next thirteen years we will lose more American infants than we have lost soldiers in all the wars fought by the nation in this century."

—National Commission to
Prevent Infant Mortality

What is more important than the health of a child? It is the foundation upon which all our efforts and programs will rest. Children in poor health cannot develop and learn. Infants born at a low birthweight run a high risk of having health problems. Nearly forty thousand American infants die each year before they reach their first birthday. That means every hour of every day we lose five babies. At least half of these deaths are preventable. We cannot afford to lose our young, and we cannot afford the price tag of treating this problem without a consistent program of prevention and education. Following are ways in which you can help.

help mothers get prenatal care

The number of infant deaths and low birthweights can be drastically reduced if mothers receive prenatal care. Participate in a program designed to provide young mothers with the care they need. You can help by encouraging mothers to seek treatment, setting up appointments, or providing transportation.

"The most precious gift we can give to children is health. But too many of America's babies are born with birth defects and low birthweight. Too many die before they even reach their first birthday. But people can make a difference. I can't think of a more important cause to volunteer for than helping to improve the health of America's babies."

—DR. JENNIFER L. HOWSE, *president*
March of Dimes Birth Defects
Foundation

The National Commission to Prevent Infant Mortality works with the public and private sectors and the media to reduce infant mortality. For information on how to help, call 202-472-1364.

The March of Dimes' annual Mother's March, held in January, includes a letter-writing campaign known as "Dear Neighbor," which delivers vital educational messages about maintaining a healthy lifestyle during pregnancy. For information, call your local chapter.

---

teach healthy habits

Limited funds and lack of education about diet and health can result in poor nutrition of mothers and low-birthweight babies. Offer to teach a class in healthy eating. Talk to the mothers about the dangers of smoking and drinking while pregnant. Contact a local youth program to set this up.

"Children are not born capable of meeting adult tasks and responsibilities. It is the task and responsibility of families and institutions to help develop children to their fullest potentials. If families are not able to do so, schools and other institutions must. Otherwise the quality of life in the society will decline, gradually at first and then precipitously and dramatically."

—James P. Comer, M.D., Yale
Child Study Center
Yale University School of
Medicine
New Haven, CT

Success by Six, a program of the United Way, strives to ensure that all children reach age six healthy and school-ready. For information on how you can help, call 703-836-7100.

Jessica, age nine

share your knowledge of children's health

Young first-time mothers often lack preparation and instruction in child care, especially in health matters. Share your parenting experience to help explain the basics of childhood health care. Beginning with the simplest matters such as preventing diaper rash, to recognizing when to call a doctor and seek medical attention, your knowledge can provide an important step to a healthier childhood. Contact a child welfare agency to become linked with a mother.

Angela, age six

support the immunization of children

According to the American Academy of Pediatrics, approximately one quarter of all American preschoolers are not fully immunized. A surprisingly high number of parents do not realize that many childhood diseases are preventable, nor are they able to afford the high costs of health care. Help spread the word about the urgency of early immunization to parents and politicians, and support the efforts of organizations that provide this basic health care precaution at little or no cost.

"While we grapple with the budget deficit, children are missing meals and measles shots; missing out on learning their colors and numbers; missing out on all the things that could make them healthy, productive adults. And in the meantime, we are running up big bills for the future in increased welfare costs, high illiteracy rates and bulging prisons."

—SENATOR CHRISTOPHER J. DODD,
chairman
U.S. Senate Subcommittee on
Children, Families, Drugs, and
Alcoholism

The National Immunization Campaign, a project of the Tides Foundation and sponsored by Children's Action Network, educates families about the importance of immunization. For information, call 310-470-9599.

Don't Wait to Vaccinate, a campaign of the Association of Junior Leagues International, promotes the early immunization of children. To get involved, call your local chapter.

offer your medical expertise

There are too few medical staff and personnel to meet the needs of impoverished communities adequately. As a health care or medical professional, you can volunteer time and provide otherwise unaffordable examinations and treatments at a community clinic. You can also contact a children's organization directly and offer to provide your medical services to the children in their programs.

"We need to dramatically expand the efforts of volunteers as change agents. We will find lasting community improvement when more citizen volunteers direct efforts toward setting community goals, developing a community infrastructure that focuses on these goals, and advocate for the policies that will sustain the infrastructure."
—HOLLY SLOAN, *president*
The Association of Junior
Leagues International, Inc.

Through The Children's Health Fund, created by singer Paul Simon and Dr. Irwin Redlener, homeless children are provided with free and consistent health care via mobile medical units. For more information, call 212-535-9400.

The National Association of Community Health Centers helps communities organize health centers and links health care professionals and others to centers in need. For more information, call 202-659-8008.

lend support at a clinic

The long wait to receive medical attention at a clinic or hospital can be stressful to parents and children. Parents often have to bring other siblings, which can make the wait more taxing. Contact the volunteer unit at a hospital or call a clinic and offer to spend time with a family in need. Read or play games with the children, and help the parents with the administrative procedures. Donating toys, games, or books to the waiting area can be very helpful.

Through Children Can Soar in Birmingham, AL, children waiting for health care treatment are provided with games and learning materials. To learn more, call 703-836-7100.

"Dr. Stubs," "Dr. Bobo," and "Dr. Celery Trashcan" from the Clown Care Unit® of the Big Apple Circus entertain children in New York hospitals. Among their ploys are bubble-blowing stethoscopes. For more information, call 212-288-2500.

arrange for an emergency care person to teach a class

Injuries are the number one killers of children. Help parents learn how to protect infants and children from harm and what to do in case of a medical emergency. Arrange for an emergency care specialist to teach this critical information at a local community program.

The National Safe Kids Campaign has coalitions nationwide that implement community-based programs to prevent childhood injury. For more information, call 202-939-4993.

help raise your community's awareness of children's health care

Many people are unaware of how serious a problem the lack of children's health care is in this country. The United States ranks eighteenth of thirty-six in infant mortality, lagging behind many developed and underdeveloped nations. Find out the facts. Invite a guest speaker from a health organization to address your group and to guide you in what you can do to improve this alarming situation.

"What we have failed to recognize up until now is that when children start out with medical, social, and educational deficits, they will be contributing to the federal deficit every day of their lives thereon."

—Representative George Miller,
chairman
U.S. House of Representatives
Committee on the Interior

Child Health Day, held the first Monday of every October, is a national symposium for legislators, health professionals, and community leaders to focus on children's health needs. To order a kit with project ideas or information, call The National Maternal and Child Health Clearinghouse at 202-625-8410.

advocate for the welfare of children with an hiv-related diagnosis

Children who are HIV-positive or who have an AIDS or ARC diagnosis need special attention to ensure adequate health care as well as a nurturing environment and normal interaction with others. Lack of knowledge creates misconception. Learn about immune-system disorders, and help educate people in your community.

"Whether you have children or not, you do have a stake in their health and well-being. Children can't vote—they have no voice, so we as adults have to be that voice. When we work to make life better for children, we're working toward a better future for all of us."
—RAE K. GRAD, executive director
National Commission to
Prevent Infant Mortality

Catholic Charities coordinates efforts in many communities to assure adequate care and attention to children with an HIV or related diagnosis. Contact your local agency to find out how to get involved.

Chanel, age eleven

advocate for a children's national health policy

Nearly ten million American children have no health insurance, and millions of others have inadequate insurance. Uninsured families tend to wait longer to seek medical care when a child gets sick, in hopes that the child will recover. This results in more serious illnesses. Access to regular health care could reduce the number of children who suffer illnesses, disabilities, and even death. Urge your local and national politicians to support creation of a children's national health insurance system.

"How we care for our children has a profound impact on whether or not they grow up to be healthy, productive adults. As a nation, we must ensure that each child has the benefit of prenatal care, regular checkups, immunizations, a healthy diet, and a safe growing environment. In this area, more than any other, a penny invested now will save us thousands of dollars in the future."

—*Representative Henry A. Waxman,*
chairman
U.S. House of Representatives
Subcommittee on Health and
the Environment

S   T   A   T   I   S   T   I   C   S

"Every day in America:

638 babies are born to mothers receiving late or no prenatal care
107 babies die before their first birthday
742 babies are born at low birthweight"

—The Children's Defense Fund

"One in ten babies in the United States is born prematurely or with low birthweight. Low-birthweight babies are forty times more likely to die in infancy than normal-weight babies. Those who live often have physical disabilities and learning disorders."

—National Commission to Prevent
Infant Mortality

"A child born in Japan, Finland, Hong Kong, Ireland, Australia, Canada, Singapore, or any of twelve other industrialized nations has a better chance of surviving his or her first year than a child born in the United States of America."

—*National Commission to
Prevent Infant Mortality*

"One in ten infants and one in five black infants living in the United States has no routine source of health care.

"The proportion of all U.S. infants and toddlers fully vaccinated against preventable disease lags behind sixteen other nations.

"One dollar spent on childhood immunization can save $10 later in medical costs.

"It costs $600 to provide pregnant women effective prenatal care to prevent a premature delivery, and it costs $1,000 per day to try to save a high-risk premature baby."

—THE CHILDREN'S DEFENSE FUND

AMERICAN ACADEMY OF
PEDIATRICS
141 Northwest Point Boulevard
P.O. Box 927
Elk Grove Village, IL 60009-
0927
708-228-5005

AMERICAN RED CROSS
431 18th Street NW
Washington, DC 20006
202-737-8300

THE ASSOCIATION OF JUN-
IOR LEAGUES
660 First Avenue
New York, NY 10016-3241
212-683-1515

CATHOLIC CHARITIES, U.S.A.
1731 King Street, Suite 200
Alexandria, VA 22314
703-549-1390

HEALTHY MOTHERS, HEALTHY
BABIES COALITION
409 12th Street SW
Washington, DC 20024-2188
202-638-5577/863-2458

MARCH OF DIMES BIRTH DE-
FECTS FOUNDATION
1275 Mamaroneck Avenue
White Plains, NY 10605
914-428-7100

NATIONAL ASSOCIATION OF
COMMUNITY HEALTH CEN-
TERS
1330 New Hampshire Avenue
NW, Suite 122
Washington, DC 20036
202-659-8008

NATIONAL CENTER FOR
HEALTH EDUCATION
72 Spring Street, Suite 208
New York, NY 10012
212-334-9470

NATIONAL COMMISSION TO
PREVENT INFANT MORTAL-
ITY
Switzer Building, Room 2014
330 C Street SW
Washington, DC 20201
202-472-1364

THE NATIONAL IMMUNIZA-
TION CAMPAIGN
c/o Children's Action Network
10951 West Pico Boulevard
Los Angeles, CA 90064
310-470-9599

NATIONAL SAFE KIDS CAM-
PAIGN
111 Michigan Avenue NW
Washington, DC 20010-2970
202-939-4993

HELPING THE PARENTS

"The program is a life saver! I'm making something of myself because it is so helpful. I wouldn't be where I am today and where I'll be in the future if it wasn't for the program."
—BERNADINE MICHAEL

"The program is a great way for all of us parents to be able to have an education and finish high school. So that we're able to go find a job to support our kids and make a better living."
—KIA VANG
participants,
Teen Parenting Program
Boulder Valley Schools
Boulder, CO

   Young mothers and fathers desperately need support. So many of them have had inadequate parenting role models and are virtually children themselves. As a result, they are left largely ill equipped—emotionally, physically, and financially—for the responsibilities of parenthood. Great numbers of young mothers without high-school diplomas are left to care for children on their own. If we can help these young people get the education, guidance, and support they need, they can begin to break the cycle and equip their children successfully for the future. This section suggests a variety of ways in which you can help.

support programs that provide comprehensive support to teen parents

Young parents need all kinds of counseling—educational and career support, help finding housing, parenting instruction, self-esteem, and leadership development. Support programs in your community that provide multifaceted services. Find out how you can help, from volunteering to fundraising to finding opportunities for young people in the community. Your local volunteer center or social service agency can recommend a program.

"To best serve our nation's children, we should seek to make our own families stronger. It's the collective strength of each healthy family that will make for a strong nation."

—GENEVA B. JOHNSON
president and chief executive
officer
Family Service America, Inc.

Family Service America, Inc., has a network of agencies that provide a variety of services designed to strengthen and support families. To locate the agency nearest you, call 800-221-2681.

The Kennebec Child Abuse Council in Maine publishes *Youth Yellow Pages, Connections to the Community,* to encourage youths to seek support. To find out how to create a guide for your community, call 207-626-3428.

---

help young parents get parenting instruction

Parent education is a powerful tool in helping new parents understand children and develop positive interaction techniques. Too often, parents treat their children the way they were treated, and patterns of abuse and neglect are continued. A parenting class can point out to mothers and fathers the importance of building self-esteem in a child, as well as help teach constructive means of discipline. Many American Red Cross chapters offer parenting instruction. If yours does, arrange to bring the class to a teen program.

"When parents get child development information along with other necessary supports, they are better able to deal with their children in ways that build the trusting, loving relationship all parents hope to have."

—BERNICE WEISSBOURD, president
Family Focus
Chicago, IL

The National Resource Center for Family Support Programs has a database of support programs for parents nationwide. To find a program in your area, call 312-341-0900.

put together an infant care package

Many parents are unable to afford even the most basic items needed to care for their newborns and infants. You can help by making a package of essential items—bottles, blankets, formula, diapers, powder, lotion, etc. Ask your friends to join you in doing the same. Contact a community or parenting program to help you locate families in need.

"We have hope for our children because most often their parents want a better life for them: strengthening their families is the best gift you can give children."

—SISTER MARY GERALDINE
Center for Family Life in Sunset Park
Brooklyn, NY

Stork's Nest, a joint project of the March of Dimes and Zeta Phi Beta Sorority, Inc., helps mothers get prenatal health care and education. Maternity clothes, diapers, and other necessary items are also provided. To find out how you can help, call your local March of Dimes.

Through Operation Stork, a project of B'nai Brith in Southern California, members throw a "shower" to collect baby gifts, which they then donate to programs to use as incentives for pregnant teens to seek prenatal care.

---

be a mentor to a teen mom

Young mothers can benefit greatly from a one-to-one relationship with a caring role model. Often they have no one they can turn to for support or advice. There are many ways you can help—sharing parenting tips, discussing infant health care, advising about careers, or just listening.

"There are so many things that are so simple to share that can make such a difference to a young mother and her child. So many of the moms have just never had anyone to show them some of the most basic things. It can take so little to point the way."

—SUSAN CARLIN, participant
Mentor Mom program
Rockford, IL

Big Brothers/Big Sisters of Northern Illinois and Rockford MELD run a Mentor Mom program to match teen mothers with women from the community. For information, call 815-965-8336.

Michelle, age twelve

be a role model for a teen father

Many young fathers have grown up without a father figure in their lives. Share your experience and lend some encouragement to them in their role as a new parent. Ask your group members, friends, or coworkers to join you. Your presence and reassurance can have an impact on the overall health of their family.

"Young, unwed fathers are perhaps one of the most forgotten human beings on the planet; but here young fathers are embraced, involved, and encouraged to be a part of the family equation."
—RICHARD BROWN, *founder*
Young Fathers Support Group,
The Valley, Inc.
New York City

The Citizens Committee for New York City will send you a booklet on how to start a support group for fathers. To order one, call 212-684-6767.

The Young Fathers Support Group at The Valley, Inc., in New York City teaches parenting skills to new fathers and encourages responsibility and involvement in their children's lives. For advice on starting a similar program, call 212-222-2110.

---

adopt a family

Be a friend to a family in need. Help them to become established in their community by directing them to local resources and helping them locate educational or recreational opportunities for their children. Families often feel isolated and are not aware of the support available to them, especially those families who have been homeless and are relocating to housing in a new neighborhood. Contact the Department of Child Welfare or local housing authority to connect you with a family.

Mary Elliot, a New York City interior designer, adopted a homeless family six years ago. She is still a friend to the entire family, helping both the mother and the children make healthy, positive choices and avail themselves to opportunities and resources within the community.

Adam, age five

lend support in preventing child abuse or neglect

According to a survey by the National Committee for the Prevention of Child Abuse, an estimated 2.5 million children were reported abused or neglected in 1990; as a result of the abuse or neglect, 1,211 died. The American Humane Association estimates that in almost 81 percent of these cases, the parent was the perpetrator of the abuse or neglect. There are programs across the country that aim to divert abuse or neglect by offering support, guidance, and information to parents. Help at one of these programs. You can work directly with a parent, join a hotline, or help administratively.

"Everyone has a role to play in preventing child abuse. You can reach out to a parent under stress and offer some respite or provide a child in need with a helping hand. If we all get involved, child abuse can be alleviated."

—ANNE COHN DONNELLY, *director*
National Committee for
Prevention of Child Abuse

The National Committee for the Prevention of Child Abuse has chapters in fifty states. To find a chapter in your area, call 312-663-3520.

The New York State Federation on Child Abuse and Neglect runs a pledge campaign called 10,000 Promises for Parents. Members of the community are asked to pledge one tangible thing to help support parents. To start a similar campaign in your community, call 518-445-1273.

be a home visitor

According to the U.S. Department of Health and Human Services, the tendency for a parent to abuse a child is higher if the parent is emotionally immature or needy, or feels isolated with nowhere to turn. Spend time in the home of parents under stress or in a high-risk category for abuse and neglect and help them develop critical coping skills. As a supportive and guiding presence, you can help parents develop healthy and appropriate responses.

"Mothers want to be good parents. Sometimes they need assistance. Teaching them how to make wise choices and thus increase their self-esteem is one way to achieve this goal. This process helps not only the mothers, but their children as well."

—LOIS ZENKEL, photographer
volunteer coordinator, The
Women's Group
New York City

The National Parent Aide Association has a listing of 650 parent aide programs across the country. To find a program in your area, call 312-663-3520.

---

give parents relief

Stress is a major contributing factor in child abuse. Giving parents some time to themselves away from their children can help reduce this stress. Offer to spend time with children while parents go out. Many organizations have "relief programs" where you can volunteer.

S   T   A   T   I   S   T   I   C   S

"Every 31 seconds an infant is born to an unmarried mother.

"Every 35 seconds an infant is born to a mother who is not a high-school graduate.

"Every 32 seconds a 15- to 19-year-old woman becomes pregnant.

"Every 64 seconds an infant is born to a teenage mother."

—The Children's Defense Fund, Leave No Child Behind

"The average age of a child involved in an abusive or neglectful situation is 7.2 years old.

"The average age of a child who dies as a result of abuse and/or neglect is 2.8 years old."
—American Association for Protecting Children

AMERICAN ASSOCIATION FOR PROTECTING CHILDREN
The American Humane Association
63 Inverness Drive E.
Englewood, CO 80112
303-792-9900

CARING FOR CHILDREN, INC.
220 Montgomery Street, Suite 429
San Francisco, CA 94109
415-391-7714

CHILD HELP USA
6463 Independence Avenue
Woodland Hills, CA 91367
818-347-7280
National child abuse hotline:
800-4-A-CHILD (800-422-4453)

FAMILY RESOURCE COALITION
200 South Michigan Avenue, Suite 1520
Chicago, IL 60604
312-341-0900

FAMILY SERVICE AMERICA, INC.
11700 West Lake Park Drive
Milwaukee, WI 53224
1-800-221-2681

NATIONAL BLACK CHILD DEVELOPMENT INSTITUTE
1023 15th Street NW Suite 600
Washington, DC 20005
202-387-1281

NATIONAL COMMITTEE FOR PREVENTION OF CHILD ABUSE
332 South Michigan Avenue, Suite 1600
Chicago, IL 60604-4357
312-663-3520

NATIONAL COUNCIL OF LA RAZA
810 First Street NE, Suite 300
Washington, DC 20002
202-289-1380

NATIONAL EXCHANGE CLUB FOUNDATION FOR THE PREVENTION OF CHILD ABUSE
3050 Central Avenue
Toledo, OH 43606-1700
419-535-3232

NATIONAL PARENT AIDE ASSOCIATION
32 South Michigan Avenue, Suite 1600
Chicago, IL 60604-4357
312-663-3520

SPEAKING UP
MAKING A
DIFFERENCE

"In our country, one of the richest in the world, every citizen's basic needs should be met. Government involvement is essential if this is to happen. We must, therefore, focus some of our energy on ensuring that our public policy provides for the needs of all our citizens."

—SHIRLEY J. POWELL
executive director
Hunger Action Coalition
Detroit, MI

" . . . as a nation, we must set a new course to save our children, strengthen their families, and regain control of our national destiny. There are no quick fixes to the problems that threaten the lives and prospects of so many of America's young people, but the solutions are within reach. I hope that our work . . . will engender the leadership, sustained commitment, and meaningful action that our children so urgently and richly deserve."

—SENATOR JOHN D. ROCKEFELLER IV,
chairman
National Commission on
Children

"If you can give people a vehicle to express their concern and compassion for children, they will respond. People are out there looking for ways to help."

—STEPHEN CAREY, founder and
director
Impact volunteer organization
New York City

A D V O C A C Y

"Our children, our society, you and I, cannot wait for tomorrow. We must act now. It is time to take off our kid gloves for children."
—MARK RILEY, director
The Children's Campaign
Child Welfare League of
America

"Never doubt that a small group of thoughtful citizens can change the world. Indeed, it is the only thing that has."
—MARGARET MEAD

Children have no voice politically and must rely on adults to represent them. The way in which we care for our children will impact and measure us as a nation for years to come. While the crisis affecting children is one of the most urgent issues facing us today, it rarely gets the attention or action it demands. We can make a difference by letting our concerns for our children be known. This section shows the steps you can take to ensure that the most basic rights of all children are met.

be informed

Know the facts about hunger, health, homelessness, and education and their impact on children. The facts and statistics are very powerful and make a persuasive case for investing in children now. Read the papers, watch the news, and be mindful of stories about the well-being of children.

"To build a society that takes everyone to a higher ground, we have to ensure that all children are given the chance not just to make it, but to excel. The ultimate challenge to each of us is to ask ourselves what we owe another human being. Nothing is more fulfilling or more essential than helping kids realize the potential inherent in every young life."

—SENATOR BILL BRADLEY,
co-chairman
Advisory Council on the Rights
of the Child

The Children's Defense Fund offers one of the strongest voices for children. For thorough research, publications, and guidance on how to advocate for policies and programs impacting on children, call 202-628-8787.

join an advocacy group

There are organizations across the country whose sole purpose is to protect the rights of children. They will supply you with all current and relevant information on children's issues. They will tell you what bills are up in Congress that need support as well as how to organize locally. Contact the Children's Defense Fund or the Child Welfare League of America.

"There are very few people who have made dramatic world changes. What we all can do is our own share to help kids in our neighborhoods, in our cities, in our states. That way we can help kids all over the country."

> —DAVID LIEDERMAN, executive
> director
> Child Welfare League of
> America

The Children's Campaign is a national network of thousands of citizens who are committed to speaking out on behalf of children. To join, call 202-638-2952.

Be drug free don't do drugs because this is what you will look like...
This is how you look when you don't do drug's or drink, you be healthly and won't stay on street

Paula, age eleven

voice your concern

Talk to your friends, coworkers, classmates, and group members about your concern for children. Speak up at functions—your company's banquet, parents' meetings, or your child's school or club meetings. Be prepared to tell people what they can do to help and where to go for information.

"The problem is just tremendous. There has got to be a massive effort on the scale of a Billy Graham crusade. In order to cut through the layers of anger and fear that surround our youth, people all across the country must do what they do best and work in collaboration."
—*Janet Barrett, founder and executive director Vehicles, Inc. New York City*

Jessica, age eight

register to vote—and vote!

This is one of the most important steps in advocating. Nothing can be accomplished without candidates in office who are concerned with children's issues. Your advocacy group can advise you about which issues to ask your candidate.

"If people did nothing other than register to vote and vote for candidates who take children's issues seriously, they would do a great deal in making a difference for children."

—Mark Riley, *director*
The Children's Campaign
Child Welfare League of
America

So You Want to Make a Difference: Advocacy Is the Key, a citizen's guide to taking action by Nancy Amidei, is available through the Office of Management and Budget Watch. To order, call 202-234-8494.

Draw people + kids with smiles because of their bandges + their hurts cured.

Love

Josephine, age fourteen

contact your local and national politicians

Calls and letters can make a real difference when a legislator is deciding on an issue. Find out from your advocacy group what bills are up for a vote, and put on the pressure. Let your local leaders know your concern about their stand on measures affecting children. They take the views of their constituents seriously.

"If you can get ten phone calls to a politician at a state level, you can create a real issue. If you get twenty, you can really make a difference."

> —ESTHER HANIG, *coordinator of public policy*
> *The Bread Project*
> *Boston, MA*

For weekly information on bills concerning children, call the Children's Defense Fund's legislative hotline at 202-622-3678.

To voice your views to the president on issues concerning children, call the White House Comment Line at 202-456-1111.

To contact your legislators, write:

Honorable_____   Honorable_____
U.S. House of Representatives   U.S. Senate
Washington, DC 20515   Washington, DC 20510

Capitol Hill switchboard:
202-224-3121

get involved in a political campaign

Help out a candidate of your choice who represents your views about children. You can get involved at any level, from answering phones in the office to canvassing in the field.

Keeping the Promise Campaign is designed to ensure that world leaders keep the promises they made at the 1990 United Nations World Summit for Children. More than twelve hundred communities in the United States have already joined. For information, call 202-546-1900.

---

write to the editor of your newspapers

It is too easy for people to forget about the plight of our nation's children. Write a letter to the editor voicing your concern. Supply them with moving facts and figures about why it is in everyone's best interest to invest in children. The Children's Defense Fund can provide you with convincing arguments and compelling statistics.

Bob Levey, a popular columnist for *The Washington Post,* has raised almost $5 million for a children's hospital through his moving editorials on the plight of the children.

be a community leader

Find out how you can participate in local government. The PTA, school board, town or city council, and community board are all accessible to the public. Decisions that affect the welfare of children often get made at the grass-roots level. People committed to making children a priority are needed to exert their influence.

"One of the strongest types of volunteerism is getting involved with grass-roots political groups. People with compassion for children must speak up at the local level."

> —Lou Trapani, *acting executive director*
> *Governor's Office for Volunteer Service*

DAWN for Children, Inc., a Rhode Island advocacy group, has a Voices for Children campaign to recruit and train citizens to lobby for children. To find out how to start a similar campaign, call 401-351-2241.

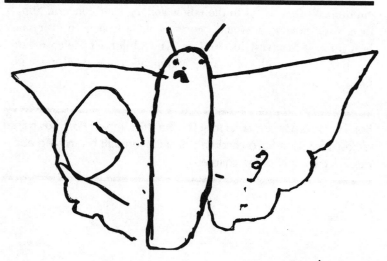

Jared, age six

get your congregation involved

Your place of worship can be a powerful arena for calling attention to the welfare of children. Ask the leaders of your congregation to encourage members to take action. Suggest projects such as a food drive, mentoring, or making calls to politicians on behalf of children.

"Children are the future of humanity. Therefore, anything that disturbs the proper training of a child is a sin against humanity. Children must be taught love by being loved. Children must be taught kindness by being treated with kindness. Children must be taught to care about others by others caring for them."
—RABBI JACOB S. FRIEDMAN
Temple Beth Torah, Ocean, NJ

The Unitarian Universalist Service Committee's Promise the Children program will send your organization or congregation information that supports education and advocacy for families and children in poverty.

Interfaith Impact for Justice and Peace encourages advocacy among religious groups. To get your group involved, call 202-543-2800. For information on congressional bills, call their weekly hotline at 800-424-7290.

CHILD WELFARE LEAGUE OF
  AMERICA
440 First Street NW, Suite
  310
Washington, DC 20001-2085
202-638-2952

THE CHILDREN'S CAMPAIGN
Child Welfare League of America
440 First Street NW, Suite
  310
Washington, DC 20001-2085
202-638-2952

CHILDREN'S DEFENSE FUND
25 E Street NW
Washington, DC 20001
202-662-3678

COALITION ON HUMAN
  NEEDS
1000 Wisconsin Avenue, NW
Washington, DC 20007
202-342-0726

INTERFAITH IMPACT FOR JUS-
  TICE AND PEACE
110 Maryland Avenue NE
Washington, DC 20002
202-543-2800
For the latest information about
  pending bills: 800-424-7290

KEEPING THE PROMISE
236 Massachusetts Avenue
  NE, Suite 300
Washington, DC 20002
202-546-1900

NATIONAL LEAGUE OF CITIES
1301 Pennsylvania Avenue
  NW
Washington, DC 20004
202-626-300

OFFICE OF MANAGEMENT
  AND BUDGET WATCH
1731 Connecticut Avenue NW
Washington, DC 20009-1146
202-234-8494

UNITARIAN UNIVERSALIST
  SERVICE COMMITTEE
Promise the Children Program
130 Prospect Street
Cambridge, MA 02139-1813
617-868-6600

S P R E A D   T H E   W O R D

"We can work together to make a difference in the future."
— *Paula Abdul, performer*

"If we can't care for children and secure for them a future filled with promise, not despair, then all the other achievements of this society will be diminished. There is no more important test of a nation's place in history than the condition of its children."
— *Tom Brokaw, Anchor, NBC*
Nightly News

Everyone can play a role in making more people aware of the plight of children and in motivating others to take action. It is important that children in need do not remain invisible. Change for children will come more quickly with widespread and unified efforts to draw attention to their needs. This section offers suggestions of how, when, and where you can take the opportunity to spread the word and make the well-being of children everyone's concern.

ask to hear the good news about young people

There are so many negative stories told about youth through the media. Yet for every "bad" story, there are many wonderful examples of young people triumphing, turning their lives around, and reaching out to help others. Let your newspapers and TV stations know you want to hear the good news. Share positive stories you know.

Bust the Stereotypes, a project of Youth Uprising in New York City, urges newspapers, TV, and radio to portray youth in a positive light. For their recommendations, call 212-684-6767.

The Giraffe Project honors people who "stick their necks out" for the common good in their communities. To nominate your local hero, call 206-221-7989.

Augusto, age seven

encourage children and teenagers to speak up

Young people have a lot to say, and we have a lot to learn from them. Ask a newspaper to feature a youth column, or a TV news show to have a youth beat hosted by a young person.

" . . . Young people [talk] about issues more intelligently and passionately than any politician or news commentator I have heard in recent memory. . . . Whether the issue is war, education, housing, the homeless, young people can be found on the front lines of change."

—Demi Moore, *national spokeswoman for the CityKids Foundation, a multicultural youth organization in New York City whose mission is to ensure that the voices of youth are heard. Her involvement has drawn great national attention and support to the program.*

JC Penney in its Golden Rule Award program recognizes voluntary community service. In selected communities throughout the United States, local winners are chosen by community leaders and publicly honored, with a contribution made to the organization for which they work.

ask the media to support volunteers

Newspapers, television, radio, and magazines can honor the endeavors of community members. This helps to remind people of how important it is to reach out and how each person *can* make a difference. The media can also provide information on where to volunteer. Seeing a specific request can be just the catalyst someone needs to take the first step.

"ABC is proud to use the power and the reach of television to increase public awareness and understanding of the expanding problems that have created a crisis situation for many of our young people, our communities, and our nation. We must come together as a nation to step up to the challenge of helping our young people."

—JAMES E. DUFFY, national
spokesperson
Project Literacy U.S.
Capital Cities/ABC, Inc.

Tom Brokaw runs a segment in the *NBC Nightly News* program called "The Daily Difference." On Tuesday evenings he highlights innovative solutions to social problems in his "What Works" segment.

The Herald Journal in Logan, UT, draws attention to its citizens who care by recognizing the "Volunteer of the Week." Their readers are also reminded of the town's volunteer opportunities by a weekly column coordinated by the local Volunteer Action Center.

television stations can help promote awareness

Millions of people can be reached by television. One program on the plight of children and on what can be done to help them can have a profound impact on what gets done. Write to your local and national TV stations requesting this kind of programming. Let them know of your positive response when programming on children at risk is aired.

" . . . Using television to mobilize volunteers for education sets the standard for responsible community programming. The response has been overwhelming. . . . I find it very moving that people are willing to give of themselves and will always find the time to help a child in school."

—SANDRA VOGEL, coordinator
Project Reach Out
Maryland Public Television
Owings Mills, MD

Lynda Guber and Carole Isenberg, former teachers turned film producers, cofounded Education First!, an organization that convinces major networks to produce programs that promote education and encourage young people to stay in school.

PBS and the United Way have formed a partnership dedicated to increasing public awareness of the crisis facing our nation's youth. They help public television stations and children's organizations use the media to create programs that focus on what can be done to help children.

get celebrity support

When a known personality gets behind an issue, it is extremely helpful in moving the entire public to get involved. Ask a celebrity to give his or her support to your event or organization for children. Celebrities can host benefits, do public service announcements, or simply lend their famous name to your cause. To get in touch with a celebrity, check *Who's Who in America* for mailing addresses.

Through The Creative Coalition, members of the entertainment industry use their access to the media to draw attention to pressing social issues. Ron Silver, Susan Sarandon, Christopher Reeve, Alec Baldwin, and Jill Clayburgh are just some of its members.

The Children's Action Network is an organization of entertainment industry leaders and others who work through the media to raise awareness of children's issues.

invite a speaker to talk about volunteering

There are people in your community who can give your group information on a variety of volunteer options. Ask your local volunteer center to recommend someone.

Lenore Skenazy, a journalist, teaches a course at the New School for Social Research in New York City called "Beyond Licking Envelopes: Volunteer Options." Volunteer directors address the audience, then meet with those interested in getting involved.

ATHLETES AND ENTERTAIN-
 ERS FOR KIDS
Corporate Headquarters
330 West Victoria Street
Carson, CA, 90248
Mailing Address: P.O. Box 191,
Building B
Gardena, CA 90248-0191
800-933-KIDS
310-768-8493

CHILDREN'S ACTION NET-
 WORK
10951 West Pico Boulevard
Los Angeles, CA 90064

Shakeal, age five

S P E C I A L

G R O U P S

S P E C I A L   D A Y S

"It is the essence of youth to recognize that all great change begins with an idealistic notion. It is the voice that says sometimes simply, sometimes movingly, sometimes inspiringly, often quietly. 'Things aren't what they should be. Things aren't what they could be, we can do better and we must try.' Young people . . . have shown me time and again if we can only tap and channel our greatest natural resource—the energy and idealism of our nation's youth—we truly could change the world."

> —ALAN KHAZEI, co-founder and
> executive director
> City Year
> Boston, MA

"When we take time to ask children what and how they want to learn and to value them as contributors, we'll go a long way towards achieving a just society, in which everyone is treated with dignity and respect."

> —CLAY THORP, co-founder
> Student Coalition for Action in
> Literacy Education

"Every volunteer makes a difference."

> —MICHELLE NUNN, executive
> director
> Hands On Atlanta
> Atlanta, GA

YOUTH REACHING OUT

"There is a movement throughout the country of young people thinking critically about issues and taking action. They are working in soup kitchens, starting tutoring programs, and developing new ways to solve community problems. Their actions may be the most hopeful signs we have for our future."
> —MAURA WOLF, youth service
> coordinator
> Points of Light Foundation

"I don't know if the world can really be changed; but one-to-one I can make a child a little happier, and that's a step in the right direction."
> —MIMO MASUDA, student
> Dalton School
> New York City

Young people are an invaluable resource—filled with energy and vitality. They have a great deal to contribute to our communities and can be a strong source of support for other children. Often all they need is to be asked to help and shown how. Developing a caring attitude and a commitment to action at an early age can help establish a pattern of involvement and concern that can last a lifetime. Reaching out carries its own rewards. The benefits for young people are increased self-esteem and confidence and the sense of having a meaningful role in the community. This chapter offers suggestions on how youth from every background can make a difference.

join a community service program at your school

Through community service, you can get involved in a wide range of projects, including mentoring, tutoring, working in a soup kitchen, or helping children at a shelter. If your school has a program, join it. If it doesn't, be active in establishing one. There are several organizations that will help you and your school set up a program.

"Students have the energy, imagination, and intelligence to make a difference in their community. They need only be asked to show what they can do."

—KATHLEEN KENNEDY TOWNSEND,
founder
Maryland Schools for Success
Baltimore, MD

Through Youth Service America, young volunteers contribute 250 million hours of public service annually. To find out what you can do or how your school can get involved, call 202-783-8855.

Seekonk High School, in Seekonk, MA, has an independent study program offering high-school seniors the opportunity to leave school for up to one day a week to do community volunteer work.

---

tutor younger students

Help students from lower grades from either your own school, or from another, do their homework or learn how to read. Not only will you be helping a child academically, but also your care and attention can make a child feel special and worthwhile.

" . . . what we keep reminding each other is that 'each one must teach one, each one must reach one, each one must bring one back into the sun.' "

> —LAURIE MEADOFF, *president and founder*
> *CityKids Foundation*
> *New York City*

StarServe has sent a kit of materials and information to every school in the country to help teachers engage students in community service. For information, call 800-888-8232.

don't smoke
in
front of
children

Cornelias, age nine

organize a drive

A school is an ideal place in which to hold drives. Decide what your concerns and priorities are—warm clothing for winter, food, toys, books, or blankets—and get your whole school involved. Each classroom can set up a bin to be filled anytime with donations. Keep track of all you give; you will be amazed at how much good you can do in one school year.

"Doing work for senior citizens, Habitat for Humanity, or whatever else there is to do gives me a better understanding and outlook on life. It gives me satisfaction just to see the smiles and sometimes the hope that we spread throughout the different communities."

—KEVIN MCCLUER, student
Grove Port Madison School
participant, The LINK Program
Grove Port, OH

Young America Cares! of the United Way encourages and supports youth community service projects. To join or to start one in your community, call your local United Way chapter or the national office at 703-836-7112, ext. 548.

plan fundraising events

Select a goal—sending one child to camp, buying sports equipment or school supplies, creating a fund for field trips, or donating to a children's program. Organize fundraisers throughout the year to help accomplish your goal. Get all the classes in your school involved.

"I remember what it was like to be a child and feel very sorry so many children aren't able to have that innocent or carefree experience."
—MARIA GARRETT, *student*
The Brearly School
New York City

Through ACTION's Student Community Service programs, students nationwide help meet community needs. To participate, contact a local Action office or call 202-606-4824.

After hearing a talk about the plight of children in New York City, Maria Garrett organized Kids for Kids, a benefit performance of high-school orchestra players, and donated approximately $5,000 to the Association to Benefit Children.

---

donate supplies

Speak with someone in the administration office at your school about "recycling" old equipment or donating excess supplies to a school in need. Many schools have inadequate budgets and are unable to afford some of the most basic items. Ask your school board to help select a school in need.

"If everybody could just find the one thing that they are good at and just do that, then that would make someone happy."

—JUSTIN LEBO, *age fifteen*

Justin Lebo has been building bikes from broken parts and donating them to children in community homes in New Jersey since he was ten years old. When he needs to purchase materials, he does his own fundraising.

Taking Drugs is Dumb!

Jorge, age ten

invite students to share your school's facilities

Speak with the director of your community service program about picking one or more afternoons a week or weekend to invite a group of children from another school to share some of your school's facilities. You could do homework together in your library, play sports in your gym, or do supervised experiments in your science lab. This works best if done on a regular basis.

"Just think of all the people who have been made happy because of some school's community service program. When our class goes out to do volunteer work, we care. We do our best because we know that it makes other people feel good. And it makes us feel great!"
—RALPH HARVILLE, *student*
Grove Port Madison School
participant, Youth Engaged in
Service (Y.E.S.) Program
Grove Port, OH

join a youth corps

Most cities have youth corps volunteer programs in which students spend one year doing community service and in return receive training, a weekly stipend, and money toward a college education. Ask your school or youth program for information.

"To help show other young people where they're headed . . . makes me believe I can do it too."

> —LINDA MCKINLEY, *student participant, YouthBuild Gadsden Gadsden County, FL*

The National Association of Service and Conservation Corps is a clearinghouse and technical assistance organization for youth corps programs. For information, call 202-331-9647.

develop your leadership skills

It is important to realize that you can make an impact and that you be able to articulate your thoughts and ideas. Learn how to take positive action about the things that concern you. Ask your school to have a leadership forum, or find a training program in your area.

"A teenager needs a leadership role in order to set goals and to share his/her opinion and ideas so that other people can benefit from it."
                    —LOUIS LOPEZ, *student*
                    participant, YouthBuild
                    Common People
                    Boston, MA

The National Youth Leadership Council provides workshops and training to empower students K–12 and in college. For information, call 612-631-3672.

Shannon, age seven

start a youth council

Put your leadership skills into action. Start a council with classmates to learn about and discuss important issues. Develop projects that will have a positive impact on your community. Hold conferences and invite students from other schools to join you.

"I hope that all adults who make decisions affecting youth can learn to involve young people in these decision-making processes. The best results for children will be achieved if instead of trying to guess what young people might want, they actually include youth in the process of making changes."

—GALEN RANSOM, *student participant, KidsBoard Seattle, WA*

Gretchen Buchenholz developed Curriculum for Social Justice to teach students how to become advocates for children and to raise awareness of homelessness and poverty. For a copy of the curriculum, call 212-831-1322.

Now under way in sixteen U.S. cities, the Nestlé Chocolate Very Best in Youth Program offers young people decision-making authority, resources, and $10,000 grants to make positive changes in their communities.

---

take on an active role in community affairs

You are the expert on youth issues. Represent yourself and your peers. Express your views at public forums, churches, town meetings, etc. Many community boards, public officials, and city agencies have youth advisory councils where your views on pending issues can be heard.

"I want to make changes. Things aren't going according to plan. Poverty, homelessness and crime, that can't be part of the plan. Things need to be said and since we the youth will be in charge one day, it's our time to speak out."

—FREEDOM TRIPODI, age fourteen
CityKids Foundation
New York City

The National PTA will help you set up a Parent-Teacher-Student Association. For information, call 312-787-0977.

The Constitutional Rights Foundation raises students' awareness of their rights and responsibilities as citizens. For information, call 213-487-5590.

spread the word

Use your school newspaper to educate students about the welfare of children in this country. Make suggestions on how each student can pitch in to help. Announce drives and other projects, and list volunteer opportunities. Commend individual students and classes for their contributions and community service.

The Hitachi Foundation offers students ideas and resources for community service, including *Today's Heroes*, a videotape celebrating the commitments of young people. To order your kit, call 202-457-0588.

The Kid's Guide to Social Action, by Barbara Lewis, is filled with ideas on how students can make a difference.

---

shout about your accomplishments

Flood the newspapers, news shows, and radio stations with positive stories about what you have accomplished. It is important for all youth in this country to gain more respect and recognition for their capabilities and contributions.

"I think we need to let young people know that they're not powerless, that there are other young people out there organizing. Change can happen for them."

—TERESA FRANCIS, organizer,
Youth Force
New York City

become a peer counselor

A teen having a hard time often feels more comfortable turning to a friend for help than to an adult. In fact, research shows that youths who are trained as peer helpers or counselors are more effective in reaching other youths than are adults. Share your knowledge and experience with a peer in need by training to become a peer counselor. You can start a peer group at your school, youth organization, or religious group.

"Teenagers often motivate other teens better than adults can. When young people learn to organize their own antidrug and prevention projects, they learn the very same skills they need to avoid substance abuse themselves. The big advantage is that instead of seeing young people as part of the drug problem, involving them allows everyone to see how they can be part of the solution."

—MICHAEL E. CLARK, executive
director
Citizens Committee for New
York City
New York City

The National Peer Helpers Association has publications and information on peer programs across the country. For information and help starting a program, call 818-240-2926.

The Youth-Reaching-Youth Project offers a model peer program, with guide, which involves young people and students in preventing and reducing alcohol and drug use among youth in high risk situations. For information, call 202-783-7949.

S   T   A   T   I   S   T   I   C   S

"In one year, teenagers gave an estimated total of 1.6 billion hours in volunteer time.

"Teens are nearly four times as likely to volunteer when asked as when they are not."

—Independent Sector, *Giving and Volunteering in the United States* (1990).

CONSTITUTIONAL RIGHTS
  FOUNDATION
601 South Kingsley Drive
Los Angeles, CA 90005
213-487-5590

MAGIC ME
808 North Charles Street
Baltimore, MD 21201
301-837-0900

NATIONAL CENTER FOR SER-
  VICE LEARNING IN EARLY
  ADOLESCENCE
Center for Advanced Study in
  Education
Graduate School and Univer-
  sity Center of the City Univer-
  sity of New York
25 West 43rd Street, Suite
  612
New York, NY 10036-8099
212-642-2946

THE NATIONAL NETWORK
1319 F Street, Suite 401
Washington, DC 20004
202-783-7949

NATIONAL PEER HELPERS AS-
  SOCIATION
P.O. Box 3783
Glendale, CA 91221-0783
919-757-4287

NATIONAL YOUTH LEADER-
  SHIP COUNCIL
1910 West County Road B
Roseville, MN 55113
612-631-3672

STARSERVE
701 Santa Monica Boulevard,
  Suite 220
Santa Monica, CA 90401
213-452-7827

STUDENT COMMUNITY
SERVICE
ACTION
1100 Vermont Avenue NW
Washington, DC 20525
202-606-4824

YOUNG AMERICA CARES
United Way of America
701 North Fairfax Street
Alexandria, VA 22314
703-836-7100

YOUTH SERVICE AMERICA
1319 F Street NW, Suite 900
Washington, DC 20004
202-783-8855

C O L L E G E S

"Before I met my mentor, I never thought about going to college. Now I've gotten to know the campus. I think it's exciting and I want to go."
—LISA, participant
Campus Partners in Learning

"There are too many children in this country who desperately need the care and attention of adults outside of their families, and in our colleges and universities there are literally thousands of students actively devoting time and energy to serve those kids. Service to the community is now a real and integral part of the college experience in America."
—SUSAN STROUD, executive director
Campus Compact

Colleges and universities have tremendous resources that can enhance the lives of children at risk. College students themselves are a great source for one-on-one or group activities. The staff, administration, and facilities can offer many forms of support to both young people and the schools that serve them. In recent years there has been a growing commitment on campuses across the nation to ensure that all children and young people are encouraged and supported in academic achievement. This section shows how you or your campus can join in these efforts.

invite students to visit your campus

Most young people at risk do not think of college as an option. Admissions offices, college students, or alumni can contact youth programs or high schools with large populations of at-risk students and invite them to tour the college and learn firsthand about admissions procedures and college life. Reaching students as early as their sophomore year can provide them with the awareness and incentive to direct their lives toward higher education.

"Colleges gain as much from partnerships as high schools—publicity, good feelings, new students coming to the college; and both college and school faculty learn new teaching strategies from working together."

> —MERLE BRUNO, associate
> professor of biology,
> Hampshire College, Steering
> Committee of
> Five College/Public School
> Partnership

Mount Holyoke College invites female students from urban high schools to spend a weekend on the campus, attending science classes and exploring college life. College students act as hosts for the weekend.

reach out to students

Personal contact with someone from a college can make the possibility of attending seem more real. Colleges can send a representative to visit a high-school class or youth program. The representative can talk to the students about college requirements, financial aid, and career possibilities. For students interested in applying, colleges can consider waiving the application fee.

"We must remember that what liberalizes a fact is the quality of the mind that deals with it. . . . Education is the use of the mind."
—VARTAN GREGORIAN, *president*
Brown University
Providence, RI

The Primary Pregnancy Prevention Program of the Children's Aid Society guarantees admission to Hunter College in New York City to every teen who completes the program and graduates from high school. The offer extends to their parents as well.

Gorka, age seven

guarantee admissions to at-risk youth

Many colleges have begun to hold and offer spaces to at-risk students who participate in youth development programs while they are in high school. The students are linked with mentors from the college who help them succeed in their studies. Once the student graduates from high school and the program, he or she is offered a space at the college. Contact the director of a youth program to discuss implementing this program.

Syracuse University has issued the Syracuse Challenge to local youths. Any student who attends a high school within the city limits, and meets certain academic requirements, will be guaranteed admission, with funding to the full extent of financial need.

Don't let the things of this world get you down.

Jerome, age eleven

form a partnership

By developing a partnership with other colleges or local businesses, you can pool resources to enhance the academic success of at-risk students from area schools. The role of a college in a partnership can be to share facilities, donate equipment, update highschool teachers on new technologies and teaching techniques, and invite students to seminars on campus.

"The greatest problem in our society today is indifference. We will always have poverty, crime, disease, and mental illness, but it is an affirmation of our humanity to work toward solutions to these problems. If we do not believe in our power to overcome these challenges, they will overcome us."

—HELEN BELLANCA, *student*
University of Michigan

The American Association of Higher Education provides information and guidance to establish partnerships. For advice, call 202-293-6440.

get involved in community service or volunteer opportunities

Most colleges do facilitate their students' involvement in community projects, including programs for children. Find out if your college has a Community Service office, or ask the Student Government Office, the Student Affairs Office, or the Office of Minority Affairs about campus projects for children.

"I have learned just as much from 'my children' as I hope I have taught them. But most of all, I hope that I have given them some hope in society and in what they can accomplish."

—AYANNA WORTHINGTON, *student*
Radcliffe University

Through Campus Compact, 250 college presidents support college students' community service efforts. For information on collaborating with a college near you, call 401-863-1119.

The Campus Outreach Opportunity League's mission is to promote and support student involvement in community service activities. To get your campus involved, call 612-624-3018.

start or join a mentoring program

If your college has a homework help or mentoring program, sign up and ask your friends to join you. If a program doesn't exist, get together a group of your classmates, contact a school, and offer to work with the children.

"I have lost faith in the strategies that do not incorporate genuine, individual human caring as a fundamental solution to any problem in our society. Mentoring is an 'intervention' as old as time and as direct as any I know to make the hurt and fear go away."

—BROOKE BEAIRD, *project director*
Campus Partners in Learning

The Student Coalition for Action in Literacy Education gets students, faculty, and administrators involved with literacy education. For information, call 919-962-1542.

Jason, age five

adopt a school

Your dormitory, fraternity, sorority, or group can adopt one classroom at a school and supply materials, plan special projects, and create a variety of opportunities for the students.

"The adoption of Woodward Elementary School has shown me if a child can put one foot forward in showing determination and perseverance, we as adults should help them in making the rest of their journey a little easier by supporting them."

—ANTOINETTE JIMERSON
career planning and placement
University of Michigan at
Dearborn

Johns Hopkins University has a partnership among its institutions, the hospitals, the university, the medical school, and Dunbar High School to help prepare minority high-school students for education and careers in health professions. The program includes a summer session, research opportunities, and on-site learning during the school year.

Adam, age five

pick a community project for your college campus

A shelter may need painting, a new child care center may need help getting built, a nursery school may be lacking books or art supplies. Get a group together and tackle one of these challenges.

"Roses are red, violets are blue, when I do my work, I think of you."
—LLOYD HARRIS, age nine
Learning Is Fun Together
program
Albion College

Alternate Spring Break was started by students at Cornell University. During breaks, rather than take vacations, students do community projects. Habitat for Humanity's Campus Chapters Department can help set up a project at your college. Call 912-924-6935, ext. 522 or 414.

Break Away in Nashville, TN, helps college students design and implement an alternate break program, as well as find projects for students in colleges across the country. For information, call 615-343-0385.

---

start a saturday ''buddy day''

Get a group of friends together and invite some young people to spend an afternoon on your campus. You could attend a sports game, go to the library and do homework, or play together in the gym. To find out about programs at other colleges, ask one of the national community service organizations.

"The time I've spent with homeless children has given me a perspective on what is important in life and reminds me that we all have something to share."

—Jonathan Patricof, student
Harvard University

Harvard University's Phillips Brooks House Association conducts nine summer day camps for over 550 children ages five to fourteen in Boston's housing developments. These summer programs get the children off the streets while providing continuity between school years.

Dr. Reuben Sorkin started an organization to enlist the universities in Miami, Florida, to offer free tickets to area youth for cultural and sports events, giving young people a chance to become familiar with college at an early age.

support children's issues

Learn about and join in local and national efforts to improve the lives of children. Invite speakers to your campus. Your voice and action can have an impact.

"Students have always been on the forefront of movements to change society. The movement to end hunger and homelessness will be successful because today's students have grown up with the problem, identified the solutions, and refuse to become numb to humanity."
—JENNIFER COKEN, *director*
National Student Campaign
Against
Hunger and Homelessness

The National Student Campaign Against Hunger and Homelessness mobilizes students on five hundred campuses in forty-five states to end these problems. To join these efforts, call 617-292-4823.

Thousands of students participate each year in Christmas in April* U.S.A.'s efforts to renovate over twenty-five hundred homes across the country. To find out how you and your college can get involved, call 202-326-8268.

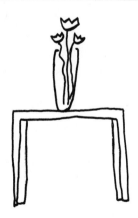

Tiffany, age nine

AMERICAN ASSOCIATION
FOR HIGHER EDUCATION
1 Dupont Circle, Suite 360
Washington, DC 20036-1110
202-293-6440

BREAK AWAY
Box 18, Peabody College
Vanderbilt University
Nashville, TN 37203
615-343-0385

CAMPUS COMPACT
c/o Brown University
Box 1975
Providence, RI 02912
401-863-1119

CAMPUS OUTREACH OPPOR-
TUNITY LEAGUE (COOL)
386 McNeal Hall
University of Minnesota
St. Paul, MN 55108
612-624-3018

NATIONAL STUDENT CAM-
PAIGN AGAINST HUNGER
AND HOMELESSNESS
29 Temple Place
Boston, MA 02111
617-292-4823

STUDENT COALITION FOR
ACTION IN LITERACY
(SCALE)
University of North Carolina at
Chapel Hill
CB 3500, School of Education
Chapel Hill, NC 27599-3500
919-962-1542

TEACH FOR AMERICA
P.O. Box 5114
New York, NY 10185
212-974-2456
800-832-1230

S E N I O R S

"I love my grandmother as much as I love my chicken."
            —R<small>ENA</small>, _age seven_
            Foster Grandparent Program

"When senior volunteers work with at-risk youngsters, wonderful, two-way relationships result. Children in need respond to the wisdom, experience, and strong family values. . . . [It's] one of our country's best examples of a successful intergenerational approach to meeting social needs."

            —N<small>ANCY</small> B<small>ETTS</small>, _director of public affairs_
            Retired Senior Volunteer Program
            Foster Grandparent Program

The talent, time, and wisdom of a senior citizen can do much to enhance the life of a child at risk. In a family under the stress of making ends meet, there is often not time for tenderness, concern, or marveling over a child's accomplishments. A caring senior can help fill this void by providing much-needed warmth, guidance, and encouragement. An intergenerational relationship can bring rich rewards to both children and seniors. This section offers suggestions on how seniors can get involved.

share your time

The presence of an older person can be a positive and stabilizing factor in a child's life. Call a children's organization to find out how you can spend time being a friend to a child who needs your attention and experience.

"No one's ever been as nice to us as our grandparents."
—*DENISE* and *STEFANIE*
Foster Grandparent Program

Senior citizens donate twenty-eight million hours annually to community projects and receive a stipend in return through the Foster Grandparent Program for low-income seniors. For information, call 202-606-4849.

Kim, age seven

be a school volunteer

You may have extra time in the afternoons when working parents are not available. You can offer a child much-needed academic support and encouragement by participating in an after-school program. Help with homework, read to a child, and help develop good study habits. Call a local school to offer your assistance. Meeting with a student even once or twice a week can give him or her the extra push needed to succeed in school.

"Children and seniors have a special kind of bonding. Seniors aren't judgmental towards the children and don't expect things the children can't measure up to. They just want to be with the children. And the children benefit from this unconditional support."

—ANNE SZUMIGALA, coordinator
Grandpersons Interested in
Volunteering in Education
(GIVE)
Toledo, OH

Through Grandpersons Interested in Volunteering in Education in Toledo, Ohio, volunteers tutor children in the schools and assist teachers and school staff. For information, call 419-246-1321.

help in a library

There is a growing trend for libraries to help meet the needs of at-risk youth by providing a safe and supportive place to do homework. Help the staff help the children. Offer to work one-on-one or with a group, and offer academic support. The soothing and concentrative atmosphere of a library can afford the opportunity to get to know a young person in a quiet way.

"In my past experiences, I have learned that a lot of love, patience, and understanding has a big effect on children. Where there is a will, there is a way. It brings me joy, working with the kids and gives me a chance to be in touch with the future."

—LOUISE W. FRUIN, Foster
Grandparent Program
Porter-Leath Children's Center
Memphis, TN

Through the Retired Senior Volunteer Program, seniors lend a hand to young people in the community. Many of their chapters run after-school programs in local libraries. For information, call 202-606-4853.

---

be a phone pal

The numbers of latchkey children are skyrocketing. Each year, more and more parents are absent from the home when their children return from school. As a phone pal, you can be the caring voice at the end of the telephone, offering help with schoolwork, sorting out squabbles among siblings, and expressing reassurance and concern.

"Kids get unconditional love from our grandmas and grandpas. They get undivided attention that parents and teachers often don't have the time to give, and we hope the connections that are made erase the misconceptions and biases that young children and the elderly have about each other."

> —Monica Glaser, *director*
> Grandma Please
> Chicago, IL

"Grandma Please" is an intergenerational helpline that links latchkey children in the Chicago area with older volunteers who are often frail or homebound. For advice on starting a phone line in your area, call 312-561-3500.

Monica, age five

volunteer at a hunger program

Food banks are frequently staffed by senior volunteers who sort food, organize distribution, or work with "gleaning" programs to salvage surplus produce from farms. Give your time to help children and their families in getting food. To participate, contact a local hunger program.

"Just thinking about helping won't make a difference. Making a commitment to taking action will. Your action will make you feel younger and more fulfilled."

> —JOHN GRANT, *public relations*
> *Senior Gleaners, Inc.*
> *North Highland, CA*

Through Senior Gleaners, Inc., senior volunteers supply more than thirteen million pounds of food to charitable organizations across the country. For information on starting a similar program in your community, call 916-971-1530.

---

when i broke my arm

Shenna, age ten

teach your skills

Many children today do not have the benefit of learning life skills that are passed from one generation to the next. Share some of your know-how. Teach cooking, sewing, carpentry, or any other special skill you have.

"I enjoy working with the teen mothers and their babies. It makes me feel good to help someone else. I hope I have instilled in the young mothers that in spite of one mistake, it's still possible to achieve their professions or goals."

> —Lucille O'Neal, Foster
> Grandparent Program
> Porter-Leath Children's Center
> Memphis, TN

lend your knowledge of business

Nonprofit and children's organizations can benefit from your business sense. From management issues to administration, marketing to planning, you can make a contribution. Ask your volunteer center to link you with an organization in need of your skills.

"It is fun—the interaction with the youngsters—and rewarding when you see the light bulb click on inside of their head."

> —Hal C. Richardson, retired U.S.
> Army engineer
> Edge Program
> Tuscon, AZ

FOSTER GRANDPARENT
  PROGRAM
  ACTION
1100 Vermont Avenue NW
Washington, DC 20525
202-634-9353

RETIRED SENIOR VOLUNTEER
  PROGRAM
  ACTION
1100 Vermont Avenue NW
Washington, DC 20525
202-634-9353

Elizabeth, age ten

HOLIDAYS AND CELEBRATIONS

"It's nice to get presents from people you don't know because it means somebody else in the world is caring about you."
—SEAN, *age sixteen*

"When they give me a present, I want to know who they are so I could thank them in person. I want them to know that whatever they buy, whether it's what I wanted or not, I'll take good care of it. I just want them to know that I'm thankful."
—NADIA, *age thirteen*
participants, Aslan Ministries
Red Bank, NJ

Holidays are times for celebrating and being thankful for what we have. They are times most children look forward to and remember for years to come. Yet for many children, Christmas is spent without toys, Easter without candy eggs, and birthdays without cake or presents. Being left out at holiday time can leave a deep imprint and add to a child's sense of isolation and loneliness. This section offers ways in which we can help make holidays as special as they should be for all our children, all year round.

make up holiday food baskets

Help a child's family have a festive meal at holiday times. Put together a holiday food basket and ask a church, social service organization, or local hunger program to locate a family in need. Coworkers, friends, and classmates can join you in delivering baskets to the families and children. This can be done at Easter, Thanksgiving, Christmas, Mother's Day, or other times throughout the year.

"I think the people who give me presents feel proud and happy. They'll be proud of theirselves for helping other people and your mom and dad."

—TANAYA, age twelve

Connect, at the First Presbyterian Church in Red Bank, New Jersey, spreads the holiday spirit by matching families to share holiday meals and friendship year round. For information on starting a similar program, call 908-530-7466.

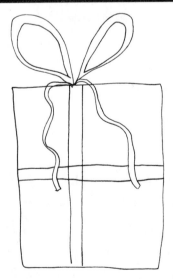

Micah, age nine

sponsor a holiday meal at a restaurant

Ask a local restaurant to open its doors to families in need at holiday time. Share costs with the restaurant and a group of neighbors and friends. Shelters or community programs can help you in inviting a group of families and children to your holiday meal. This is a way for families who often feel forgotten to feel welcome and remembered.

At the annual "Breakfast with Santa" of the Junior Auxiliary of Vicksburg, MS, children referred by the Department of Human Services are treated to live music, comedy, gifts, and a visit with Santa.

Josh, age thirteen

help make holiday decorations

It doesn't have to cost a lot to make a holiday festive. Boughs can be wrapped with ribbons, stockings can be made with felt and glitter, Valentines can be made from doilies and red paper. Hard-boiled eggs can be painted and decorated. Offer to bring some supplies to a shelter or community program, and join the parents and children in making decorations.

do something nice for a mother

Remembering a mother on a holiday can give an unexpected but much-needed treat. Mothers are often forgotten at these times. Send one rose, or put together a package of nicely wrapped soaps for one or more young mothers. Get the children involved in some respect. This is an especially nice thing to do for Mother's Day.

"Sometimes I get pretty low about not having anything for myself. . . . I feel grateful that somebody would think about me."
—TASHA, mother of two
living in a shelter

remember children's birthdays

Many children, especially those living in group homes, do not get to celebrate their birthdays. There may be no one to remember them, or a lack of sufficient funds. Start a Birthday Present Fund for children in a group home, shelter, or community program. Ask your friends to join you. Providing cake, decorations, and games can help create a real birthday.

"Teenagers in residential or group homes need some extra attention on their birthdays. Usually there are no resources for gifts and they have neither foster nor birth parents to acknowledge them."
—ANNETTE F. NELLIGAN
Children's Services supervisor
state of Maine

host a party

Instead of the usual holiday office party, why not host a party for children? This can be done on your premises, or by bringing the celebration to a children's organization. Bring presents, refreshments, and holiday cheer. Doing this at holidays throughout the year—an Easter egg hunt, a Fourth of July picnic, a Valentine's Day party—can launch relationships with the children and their families.

Coach Leatherware Company threw a party for the children at Rosie and Harry's place of the Association to Benefit Children in New York City. Coach received the name, age, and wish list of each child and parent, and employees, dressed as Santa's elves, distributed the presents during a festive meal.

Pennywhistle Toys in New York City took employees and their families to the Children's Aid Society's Big Apple Circus benefit, which helped provide medical care for homeless children.

Michael, age twelve

ask local stores to donate proceeds from holiday sales

Encourage your local stores or mall to pick one day during holiday times to give a percentage of sales to a children's organization. Get publicity for this event. This is a good way to get the whole community involved. It can also enhance business and let people know a company cares.

"It would be just so wonderful to know that the first Sunday of each December would be dedicated, nationwide, to children in need. After all, every city and town has its own shopping districts, streets or malls. Each and every one of us could truly make a difference in the lives of all the children so in need of our hope and our help."

—MARTHA DUPEE, co-founder
Madison Avenue Christmas for
Children Fund
New York City

At the Madison Avenue Christmas for Children Fund in New York City, merchants donate 20 percent of every sale one day in December to designated children's organizations. One year they donated more than $400,000. For guidance in setting up a similar event, call 212-988-4001.

organize or make a donation to a toy drive

Get your group, class, or coworkers into the holiday spirit. Set up a toy drive. Pick a children's organization to benefit. Let everyone know where to bring their present. Get together to wrap the gifts and take them to the organization.

"I suggest donating a toy to forgotten children through Toys for Tots. They accept toys all year long, not only for the holidays. When you're out buying a gift—whether for a birthday, or something from Santa— buy an extra little something for the children."

—BROOKE SHIELDS, spokesperson, Toys for Tots

Each holiday season, K mart's Needy Children's Shopping Spree offers forty-four thousand children, identified by civic organizations, $20 worth of merchandise, breakfast, and a present from Santa.

More than eight million toys a year are collected annually for children in need by Toys for Tots. To make a donation, to volunteer your services, or to sponsor a drive, call the Marine Corps Reserve Toys for Tots Foundation at 716-874-8994.

be santa claus to a group of children

Help make children's Christmas wishes come true. Ask a local shelter or children's program to have their children send "wish lists" to Santa—and you and your group answer them.

"People . . . that do things like that are people that love everybody in the world, because if they didn't love everybody in the world they wouldn't just buy a stranger a present. A lot of things I've gotten I really needed and it was a blessing in disguise."
—Larry, age eight

Through Operation Santa Claus, sponsored by the New York Post Office, children's letters to Santa are answered by caring people from all over the country. In one year more than thirty thousand children received Christmas gifts. To become a Santa Claus, call 212-967-8585.

Victoria, age seven

start a ''gift bank''

Helping parents be the bearers of gifts can make them feel good about themselves and their ability to give to their children. Get together with your church, synagogue, school, or community group to gather gifts that can be "purchased" by families in need at no cost. Ask your local retailers and manufacturers to pitch in and donate merchandise. Find a place to set up your "store," and ask social service agencies or community programs to send you "customers."

"The store lets the folks who volunteer have their eyes open to the realities of being poor and it explodes the stereotypes about who the poor really are. They are not able-bodied men, but women and children who are struggling to stay alive."

—REVEREND BILL KING, *coordinator*
Montgomery County Christmas Store
Lutheran campus pastor,
Virginia Tech
Blacksburg, VA

At the Montgomery County Christmas Store in Virginia, thousands of volunteers clean, stock, set up, and staff a vacant store filled with donated goods that families in need can purchase with points rather than cash.

send holiday cards designed by children

Ask a local children's organization that has an arts program to provide drawings by the children. You can print these to send as your holiday greeting card in exchange for a donation to the program. On the back of the card explain the work that the organization does and that you are supporting it. This is a good way to show children's talent and to bring recognition to a good organization.

"I wish for toys for my family. I wish for paper, too. I wish for clothes for my family."

> —NAHIA, participant
> Creative Arts Workshop
> New York City

Children at the Creative Arts Workshop designed holiday cards for Victor Capital Group, a New York real-estate company, which in turn made a generous donation to support the program's efforts.

make a donation

Rather than give the usual holiday or birthday gift, make a donation to a children's organization in the name of a friend, relative, or colleague. This is a particularly good idea for businesses. The organization can send out a card or letter letting the recipient know how much the gift is appreciated and how it will be used.

"I am glad when I get things but then I think how people feel without toys. I sometimes wish they had my things."

> —LEAH, age eight
> Shawnee, KS

give this book

The information in this book might be just the catalyst your friends or associates need to get involved. By giving this book to one person you can help touch the lives of many.

THE HOLIDAY PROJECT
P.O. Box 6347
Department STC
Lake Worth, FL 33466-6347
407-966-5702

TOYS FOR TOTS
Marine Corps Reserve
Joint Public Affairs Offices
4th MARDIV/4TH MAW
New Orleans, LA 70146
504-948-1227

Dashawn, age six

ADDITIONAL NATIONAL ORGANIZATIONS

ACTION
Office of Public Affairs
1100 Vermont Avenue NW
Washington, DC 20525
202-606-4855

Action is a federal domestic volunteer agency that enables people of all ages and from all walks of life to volunteer their services where needed. More than 477,000 citizens give their time to Action programs, which are dedicated to developing lasting solutions to the challenges of crime, hunger, poverty, illiteracy, drug abuse, and homelessness. The diversity of Action programs allows for part-time or full-time service, with some participants receiving stipends.

Association of Jewish Family and Children's Agencies
P.O. Box 248
Kendall Park, NJ 08824-0248
908-821-0909
800-634-7346

Volunteers for Jewish Family and Children's Agencies provide a number of services for their communities, including providing family counseling, offering job assistance, collecting and delivering food, and providing tutoring to children.

Contact Center, Inc.
P.O. Box 81826
Lincoln, NE, 68501
402-464-0602

The Contact Center is a national information and referral agency for human services; it can link individuals to programs that help youth at risk throughout the country.

Four-One-One
7304 Beverly Street
Annandale, VA
22003
703-354-6270

Four-One-One is a clearinghouse for information on community and national volunteer organizations as well as a host of other organizations that serve people in need. They will provide references and other information on how to implement and manage successful volunteer programs. The organization maintains a library of three thousand volumes and sponsors charitable programs including Super Volunteers, which encourages young people to get involved.

Points of Light Foundation—
The Volunteer Center
736 Jackson Place
Washington, DC 20503
202-408-5162

The Points of Light Foundation promotes community service for many serious social issues, including children's, by enlisting the media to raise awareness of the importance of volunteering, by mobilizing institutions to engage their members in community service, and by recognizing and encouraging community service ideas that work. They are a resource center for information, training, and assistance in designing and developing volunteer programs, corporate and otherwise. The foundation has access to the more than 380 volunteer centers in communities throughout the country that link interested parties to local volunteer opportunities.

United Black Fund, Inc.
1012 14th Street NW,
Suite 300
Washington, DC 20005
202-783-9300

The United Black Fund, Inc., can provide volunteers with a comprehensive list of organizations meeting the unmet needs of

African Americans in their communities. The organization can make recommendations for service involving child care, literacy, crime prevention, drug and alcohol prevention, and support and companionship for youth.

> United Way of America
> 701 North Fairfax Street
> Alexandria, VA 22314
> 703-836-7100

United Way acts as a catalyst to solve community problems, assessing community needs, creating and supporting programs, and mobilizing citizens to get involved. More than ten million volunteers and forty thousand United Way agencies address issues such as alcoholism and drug abuse, health research, foster care, job training, services for women, and much more. The organization links people in need with essential services and also is a resource for information on mentoring and volunteerism.

ARTS ACKNOWLEDGMENTS

The artwork in this book has been generously contributed by children throughout the country whose lives are being enhanced by the efforts of the following programs:

Arts Connection
Arts in Education, New
Orleans Public Schools
6048 Perrier Street
New Orleans, LA 70118
504-899-6441

The Arts Connection brings professional artists in the visual arts, creative writing, theater, and dance into New Orleans public elementary schools. The artists spend two and a half days a week throughout the entire school year developing partnerships with teachers and students. Programs are geared to stimulate curiosity and excitement and to emphasize the importance of children's imagination and the creative process.

Association to Benefit
Children
316 East 88th Street
New York, NY 10128
212-831-1322

This organization provides a variety of facilities and services to strengthen and meet the needs of homeless and handicapped children and their families. Comprehensive support is provided through their day care center, transitional housing, health services, and tutoring and recreation programs. They have created classroom materials to introduce issues of social justice to schools throughout the country.

I Am That I Am
Training Center
P.O. Box 41614
4937 Veterans Drive
Dallas, TX 75241
214-372-6838

I Am That I Am is dedicated to improving the outcomes of the lives of abused and neglected children and young people living in poverty and with substance-abusing parents. Through a variety of educational and support programs, it works to combat illiteracy, teen pregnancy, drug abuse and delinquency. According to its founder, Delores Beall, "It's time to take the responsibility of our children out of the hands of drug dealers and into the hands of those who care."

Creative Arts Workshop
for Kids, Inc.
625 Broadway, 2nd Floor
New York, NY 10012
212-475-8043

The Creative Arts Workshop (CAW) is designed to enhance self-esteem and direction in homeless children. Through visual and performing arts workshops as well as leadership development programs, and family support and counseling children begin to realize their abilities and strengths. CAW also provides meals, clothing, books, homework help, and holiday gifts to its participants.

Family Care Center
1135 Red Mile
Place
Lexington, KY
40504
606-288-4040

This program provides child care, education, health, and social services for up to two hundred children. They also provide support to their parents. The goal of the center is to guide children and their families toward self-sufficiency.

Faith Children's
Home
P.O. Box 22789
Tampa, FL 33622
813-961-1214

The Faith Children's Home is a Christian home for homeless and abused children between the ages of four and sixteen. Education and recreational activities are a part of the program where children stay for a minimum of twenty-four months while an attempt is made to rebuild their families.

The Family Place
4211 Cedar Springs
#100
Dallas, TX 75219
214-559-2170

The Family Place offers support and assistance to battered women and their children. They provide shelter, counseling, and outreach services. Its children's therapeutic program has become a national model. The goal of the organization is to break the cycle of family violence.

Learning through Education in the Arts Project (LEAP)
1409 Bush Street
San Francisco, CA 94109
415-775-5327

LEAP connects artists and architects with over 7,000 children in 23 San Francisco schools. Seven and eight week programs bring artists to each class for two to three hours per week to explore visual arts, dance, opera, theater, storytelling, multi-media arts, and architecture.

New Community After School and Advocacy Program
614 S Street NW
Washington, DC 20001
202-232-0457

This program strives to instill in children living in high-risk neighborhoods with a sense of pride in self, family, and heritage, and to open their eyes to the world outside their community. Working together with parents, teachers, and the community, the program helps children develop their interests and talents.

New Orleans Summer-bridge
1903 Jefferson Avenue
New Orleans, LA 70115
504-896-8595

New Orleans Summerbridge prepares 6th and 7th graders for the demands of rigorous schools. The program serves motivated, high-potential students from public and parochial schools around the city. Using talented high school and college students as teachers, the program provides two academically stimulating summer sessions. School-year tutoring, counseling, and enrichment ensure comprehensive support.

Urban Gateways: The Center for Arts in Education
105 West Adams Street, 9th Floor
Chicago, IL 60603
312-922-0440

Urban Gateways is the largest and most comprehensive arts-in-education organization in the nation. It uses the arts to enhance education, build children's self-esteem, and broaden multicultural perspectives. The organization's corps of three hundred and fifty professional artists brings dance, music, theater, and visual arts programs to nearly one million children, teachers, and parents each year.

Young Artists and Company, Inc.
18955 Warrington
Detroit, MI 48221
313-883-2626

Young Artists and Company, Inc., is a fine-arts program for inner-city youth, offering art classes and workshops taught by professional artists to all age levels. Work by young artists in the program has been exhibited at the State Capitol of Michigan and at the Museum of African American History. The program introduces young artists to art-related careers. It also encourages its participants to do community service by creating exhibitions to aid other nonprofit organizations.

BIBLIOGRAPHY

Amadei, Nancy. *So You Want to Make a Difference: Advocacy is the Key.* Washington, DC: OMB Watch, 1991.

The Annie E. Casey Foundation. Focus: A Quarterly Report from the Annie E. Casey Foundation. Greenwich, CT: The Annie E. Casey Foundation, Fall 1991.

Aspira Association. Aspira: Building Leadership to Build the Future. Washington, DC: Aspira Association, 1990.

Big Brothers/Big Sisters of America. Big Brothers/Big Sisters of America 1990 Annual Report. Philadelphia, PA: Big Brothers/Big Sisters of America, 1991.

The Business Roundtable. The Business Roundtable. New York: The Business Roundtable, 1989.

Campus Compact. Campus Compact: The Project for Public and Community Service. Providence, RI: Campus Compact, 1989.

Center for Corporate and Education Initiatives. Across The Board: The Conference Board Magazine. Waltham, MA: Center for Corporate and Education Initiatives, 1991.

Child Welfare League of America. Child Welfare League of America 1990 Annual Report. Washington, DC: Child Welfare League of America, 1990.

Children's Defense Fund. Child Poverty in America. Washington, DC: Children's Defense Fund, 1991.

———. *Leave No Child Behind: An Opinion Maker's Guide to Children in Election Year 1992.* Washington, DC: Children's Defense Fund, 1991.

———. *The State of America's Children: 1990.* Washington, DC: Children's Defense Fund, 1990.

———. *The State of America's Children: 1991.* Washington, DC: Children's Defense Fund, 1991.

Commission on Children. Beyond Rhetoric: A New American Agenda for Children and Families. Washington, DC: Commission on Children, 1991.

The Enterprise Foundation. Crossing New Thresholds. Columbia, MD: The Enterprise Foundation, 1990.

Extension Review, Winter 1990. Washington, DC: U.S. Department of Agriculture.

Foster Grandparent Program. Where Love Grows. Washington, DC: Foster Grandparent Program, 1991.

Henry, Sarah M, and D. M. Kline III. *Growing Up at Risk.* Dubuque, IA: Kendall/Hunt Publishing Company, 1990.

Hewett, Sylvia Ann. *When the Bough Breaks.* New York: Basic Books, 1991.

Illinois Maternal and Child Health Coalition and the Illinois Caucus on Teenage Pregnancy. Our Drug War Challenge: Women & Children in the Crossfire. Illinois: Illinois Maternal and Child Health Coalition and the Illinois Caucus on Teenage Pregnancy, 1991.

Independent Sector. *Giving and Volunteering in the United States.* Washington, DC: Independent Sector, 1990.

Kellogg, W. K., Foundation. *Programming for the '90s: The Continuity of Change.* Battle Creek, MI: W. K. Kellogg Foundation, 1990.

Kenyon, Thomas, with Justine Blau. *The National Alliance to End Homelessness: What You Can Do to Help the Homeless.* New York: Fireside Books, Simon & Schuster, 1991.

Kozol, Jonathan. *Rachel and Her Children.* New York: Fawcett Columbine, 1988.

————. *Savage Inequalities.* New York: Crown Publishers, 1991.

Let's Do It Our Way: Working Together for Educational Excellence. Columbia, SC: South Carolina ETV, 1991.

Lewis, Barbara A. *The Kids' Guide to Social Action.* Minneapolis, MN: Free Spirit Publishing, 1991.

March of Dimes Birth Defects Foundation. Babies and You. White Plains, NY: March of Dimes Birth Defects Foundation, 1991.

Massachusetts Community Childhood Hunger Identification Project. Children Are Hungry in Massachusetts. Boston: Project Bread, 1991.

Mnookin, Robert H. *In the Interest of Children: Advocacy, Law Reform, and Public Policy.* New York: W. H. Freeman and Company, 1985.

Mott, The Charles Stewart, Foundation. *A State-By-State Look at Teenage Childbearing in the U.S.* Flint, MI: The Charles Stewart Mott Foundation, 1991.

National Charities Information Bureau. *Wise Giving Guide.* New York: National Charities Information Bureau, 1991.

The National Collaboration for Youth. *Making the Grade: A Report Card on American Youth.* Washington, DC: The National Collaboration for Youth, 1991.

The National Committee to Prevent Infant Mortality. *Death Before Life: The Tragedy of Infant Mortality.* Washington, DC: The National Committee to Prevent Infant Mortality, August 1988.

The National Directory of Children, Youth & Families Services 1991–92. Longmont, CO: Marion L. Peterson, 1991.

New York State Communities Aid Association. *Program Review and Outlook.* New York: New York State Communities Aid Association, 1990–91.

The Ounce of Prevention Fund. *Child Sexual Abuse: A Hidden Factor in Adolescent Sexual Behavior.* Chicago: The Ounce of Prevention Fund, 1987.

Police Athletic League of New York City. *Police Athletic League of New York City.* New York: Western Publishing Group, 1989.

QED Communications and United Way of America. *A Youth Mentoring Program Directory.* Fairfax, VA: QED Communications and United Way of America, 1990.

Reading Is Fundamental. *Reading Is Fundamental.* Washington, DC: Reading Is Fundamental, 1991.

The Robin Hood Foundation. *The Robin Hood Foundation.* New York: The Robin Hood Foundation, 1991.

Shelton, Cynthia W. *The Doable Dozen. A Checklist of Practical Ideas for School-Business Partnerships.* Alexandria, VA: National Community Education Association, 1987.

Smith, Thomas J., Gary Walker, and Rachel A. Baker. *Youth and the Workplace.* Philadelphia, PA: Public/Private Ventures, 1987.

Struntz, Karen A., and Shari Reville. *Growing Together: An Intergenerational Sourcebook.* Washington, DC: American Association of Retired Persons and the Elvirita Lewis Foundation. Palm Springs, CA: 1985.

Volunteers of America. This Is VOA. New York: Volunteers of America, 1990.

The White House Office of National Service. A Thousand Points of Light. Washington, DC: The White House Office of National Service, 1991 and 1992.

Wilbur, Franklin P., and Leo M. Lambert. *Linking America's Schools and Colleges: Guide to Partnerships and National Directory.* Washington, DC: American Association for Higher Education, 1991.

Neglect Not The Children, a one-hour documentary for PBS, portrays how support and guidance from caring individuals and community programs can help children and youth at risk turn their lives around. Hosted by Morgan Freeman, the film focuses on one exemplary program in New York City and its positive affects on the lives of four young people. To order a VHS copy of the film, contact the Neglect Not The Children Project, 750 Lexington Avenue NY, NY 10022. Special rates are available for schools, community programs, and organizations.

I N D E X